The dedication of this book is to Dee, who has been an inspiration from day one. Without her brilliance as a mother, none of this would have been possible.

Ice Rider

ISBN - 978-1-8380209-6-5

Copyright © Paul Gaskill 2020

The right of Paul Gaskill to be identified as the author of this work has been asserted in accordance with the Copyright, Designs and Patents Act 1988

All rights reserved. No part of this publication may be reproduced, stored in a retrieval system, or transmitted in any form or by any means, electronic, photocopying, recording or otherwise, without the prior permission of the author or the publisher

Published in 2020

Illustrations by Analdo Arscott

*Please visit **www.paulgaskill.co.uk***
for more details about the author and his books.

Ice Rider

The Oracus Series

Book Number Two

Paul Gaskill

Contents

1 – A New Rider ... 1
2 – The Healer ... 6
3 – Refugees Of Tallarin ... 11
4 - Sarvon ... 20
5 – Alu'reath ... 30
6 – Ulatori Culture ... 39
7 – Sparring To The Death ... 46
8 – Human Extinction ... 55
9 – Danzig's Defeat ... 65
10 – Improving A Power ... 71
11 – Saving A Life ... 80
12 – Inirił's Rage ... 87
13 – Ice And Snow ... 95
14 – Malum ... 105
15 – Ice Prison ... 117
16 – Hiding An Army ... 131
17 – Battle Of Fervia ... 147
18 – Jowra's Powers ... 160
19 – The Emerald Pairing ... 168
20 – Return To Afarra ... 175
21 – Nivin ... 183
22 – Old Friend, New Friend ... 191
23 – Revisiting The Past ... 204
24 – The Wise And The Inventive ... 215
25 – Multi-Powered ... 226
26 – Aspiring Associates ... 232

27 - Unfathomable Secret ... 240
28 - Fervia's New Inhabitants ... 246
29 - Casualties Of War ... 254

ONE

A New Rider

Wravias and Pseubas circled the sky, their giant, metal wings billowing clouds of snow over Melzor. Their silver armoured scales were spattered with snowflakes, while their crimson eyes pierced the gloomy weather, searching for any helpless creatures they might devour. The screeches of the Dragons made the ears of mere mortals bleed, but the sound filled King Jowra with an icy pleasure.

Tallarin's mighty wall had been breached, and the city itself had fallen. And that was why Jowra appeared so delighted. The battle had only cost him three-thousand men and his daughter; it was a very worthwhile sacrifice that almost certainly ensured the demise of the rebellion.

The rebels would never have dethroned him anyway, that much he was sure of. If they had somehow defeated his vast armies, he would have destroyed them all himself. He was a Vassath Rider after all, with two Dragon Lavorians. He was the most powerful man in the land by far.

Yet despite his unequalled power, a *boy* called Oracus was his only concern. Oracus was his grandson – the son of his dead daughter – and he was a Vassath too, a rare kind of Rider able to use more than one power.

There was a rumour the boy had died during battle. Gravaz the Ulatori claimed to have killed both him and his Lavorian, before throwing their bodies into the ocean. But Jowra was wise enough not to trust the empty boasts of his minions. If he assumed incorrectly that the boy had met his death, then he would be sure to regret it. The boy would grow stronger in his absence – just like Jowra himself had in the Black Forest – and there would then be a chance of him rivalling his King. Until Jowra saw his grandson's dead body with his own eyes, he would never rest.

The city of Melzor was bitterly cold, as always. A white blanket of snow covered the ground, and more flakes continued to fall from the churning grey sky. There was frost tickling the edges of the palace windows, and the deep lake in the grounds was protected by a thick sheet of ice.

The climate on this side of the Great River was the exact opposite of that on the other side. Through the window of the highest, northern-most spire in his palace, Jowra could see where the snowfall and ice were replaced by warmth, sunshine and desert. He hated the heat. So much so he had promised to one day turn the whole of Pharia into an icy bliss. With the rebellion on the brink of doom, maybe that day would come soon.

Within the window through which he observed, Jowra could see his own ghostly reflection staring back at him. His appearance hadn't changed much in the sixty years of his reign. His skin was still pale and waxy, his hair long and greasy, and his nose crooked and long above a thin mouth. But his eyes were no longer the electric blue they once were – all the hatred inside him had turned them as red as blood.

Jowra turned from his reflection, spinning his cloak through the air, and moved hastily to the door. Quent had arrived in Melzor – the coward who had been his spy inside Tallarin, and who had proven himself to be far more competent than Jowra had ever expected. For his loyalty, Jowra intended to reward him handsomely.

So Jowra headed for the long spiralling staircase that would take him to the lower levels of his palace. The staircase was dancing with shadows as he descended, and draughts of cold air whistled through the corridors that followed. Dim lamps flickered as Jowra strode by with his cloak gliding behind him, each one extinguishing with a snap of his fingers.

He reached the dungeons of his palace and entered a chamber where Quent was waiting. A lone Eevek sentinel in a scarlet robe was guarding the chamber door, faceless behind its drooping hood. Its long fingers squeezed its wooden staff as Jowra arrived, and it bowed its head respectfully.

The chamber beyond was brighter than the staircases and corridors. It wouldn't normally be so, but this chamber housed an Orbular that had fallen in the lands to the south and been brought to the King for his use. The Orbular glowed with an amber warmth that ran through its polished surface and highlighted the thousands of rat bones on the floor. It looked fragile, like an egg, but Jowra knew it to be harder than rock. A smile briefly caught the edges of his mouth.

Quent stood quiet and rigid in the corner, his cowardice there for all to see. At the sight of Jowra, he dropped to both knees and began to sob. "My King," he offered without looking up.

"Stand!" Jowra commanded him. "I'm not here to chop off your head."

Quent quickly did as he was told, but his legs threatened to buckle again. When he looked at his King, he was freckly and fearful.

"Of all my servants, it is you who has impressed me most," Jowra said truthfully. "For that, you will be rewarded."

Quent's expression eased somewhat and his eyebrows arched attentively.

Jowra pointed to the Orbular. "The rebellion has been weakened, and I want you to help bring it to its end. This is my gift to you."

Quent's mouth dropped open. "My King. Are you sure?" he gasped.

"You'd do well to bond with it before I change my mind," Jowra said impatiently.

Gingerly, Quent walked to the Orbular and studied its beauty closely. It appeared to pulsate with him so near. He reached out a hand and ran his dexterous fingers over its smooth surface, then an explosion of silver light flooded the chamber. Jowra covered his eyes with a hand until the light dimmed, and when it did, he saw Quent knelt between two halves of the broken Orbular, cradling a flawless Lavorian – a Bull calf.

It was peaceful in the chamber for a moment. Then Quent stood and a violent surge flowed through his body. His eyes glowed malevolently, and the veins in his temples throbbed with power. With a scream of delight, he raised his hands above his head and produced a magical sword in each of his fists – both made of light that matched the crimson colour of Jowra's eyes.

Quent laughed maniacally and slashed the swords through the air in front of him with speed and precision. He was no longer the coward who had spied on Tallarin. He was now a Rider.

TWO

The Healer

The vines gave way to a jagged knife and Oracus tumbled heavily to the snowy ground. There was hissing all around him as the villagers vented their disapproval of his life being spared. He was naked and cold, but grateful to the leader of the village for being merciful. When he groaned at the pain in his legs and back, two Ulatoris grabbed his arms and dragged him across the square, before throwing him headlong into an old wooden hut.

He was in the Ulatori village of Valaroth, having been captured by the grey-skinned folk in the depths of their Black Forest. They were a strong, muscular race, all twice the size of a Human, and they seemed particularly hostile towards outsiders.

Oracus was in no fit state to escape the village either. The injuries to his back and legs were substantial, and his connection to Bandor had somehow been lost too. After defeat in the battle for Tallarin, and the subsequent hours spent drifting aimlessly upon the ocean, Oracus was both physically and mentally broken. And now he had agreed to find Gravaz, a traitorous Ulatori who serves King Jowra, and bring him back to Valaroth in return for his own life being spared.

But Oracus would not simply be sent on his way and trusted to meet the agreement. Sarvon, the Ulatori leader, had said he would keep Oracus in Valaroth until he was sure he was cooperative and capable of meeting their demand. And who knew what that entailed. All Oracus knew was that he'd need to be healed first.

The hut Oracus found himself in was dim and cold, with a boarded floor and wooden rafters overhead. There was an uncomfortable stone bed he was forced to sit on, and all around the walls there were bowls on shelves, most containing herbal concoctions of some sort. In the centre of the hut, a near-bare Ulatori woman stood alone. She was scary looking, as all the Ulatoris were, and her size seemed to fill the room. She had countless piercings on her face, including a sharp bone through the ridge of her nose.

"He needs healing, Shurgda," Sarvon boomed from the hut's entrance.

Shurgda nodded her head once. Wordlessly, she lowered her enormous body onto a rickety three-legged stool beside Oracus and studied his body. When she reached out a hand, he flinched, but a sharp glare from Shurgda stopped him moving again. The Ulatori was surprisingly gentle for her size, lightening her touch at Oracus's gasps of pain and humming quietly. At first glance, Oracus had expected her to be a brute, but she was in fact quite the opposite.

"His wounds are severe," Shurgda said, her voice almost hypnotic. "It will take time."

"Summon me when it is done," Sarvon said. He flashed a glance at Oracus before retreating from the hut.

"You are hurt badly," Shurgda whispered calmly to Oracus. "How did you get injuries like these?"

"There was a battle in Tallarin," Oracus answered, surprised by the Ulatori's curiosity. "I was fighting."

"Healing you will not be a painless process," she explained.

"But I can be healed?" Oracus asked hopefully.

"Yes," she assured simply.

Oracus sighed his relief. If he'd had wounds like these back in Thessley then he wouldn't have survived. Nobody there had ever needed much skill with medicine. But just as his health worries were alleviated, new concerns came to him. Like how he would survive in a village full of savages. Whether he would ever see his friends again. And where Bandor had been taken, for he still couldn't feel the Lion's mind.

He looked at Shurgda as she dabbed his cuts with a damp cloth. "Am I safe here?" he asked, hoping for confirmation from the one Ulatori who didn't seem to hate him.

"Yes," she answered without looking up.

"I won't be killed by those out there?" He pointed to the door.

"If Sarvon wanted you dead then he would have killed you already," Shurgda replied candidly. She stood and collected a bowl from one of the shelves. It contained an odorous brown liquid.

"But Sarvon said I must prove my competence if I want to live," Oracus responded.

Shurgda splashed the liquid onto Oracus's cuts and burns. It stung terribly and he whimpered.

"You are competent," she said.

"How do you know?" Oracus asked with a grunt as his skin continued to burn.

"You are a Rider, are you not?"

"Yes, I am," Oracus conceded. He looked at his wounds and saw them sizzling beneath the medicine. Still the pain came. "But why does that make me competent?"

Shurgda lifted her head and her deep yellow eyes studied his for a few seconds. "I would have thought that was obvious," she said.

Oracus frowned and hoped she'd explain further, but she quickly returned her attention to his wounds, so he pressed on with another question. "Sarvon also said I will be trained. Do you what I'll be doing?"

"I know nothing more than how to heal," Shurgda replied. "But you will find out soon enough. And you will see how great a trainer Sarvon is."

Oracus thought back to Shio, who had been a great trainer himself. And an illustrious commander to Tallarin's army. But now Shio was dead because of Oracus's inability as a Rider. If only he had teleported them both out of the falling watchtower and not just himself. A feeling of dread washed over Oracus as he surmised that any mistakes here would likely get him killed.

"The cuts are easy to heal," Shurgda said as Oracus's pain finally lessened and his wounds sizzled no more. She mopped dirt and dried blood from his skin with the damp cloth. "But the injuries to your legs and back will be much more unpleasant to repair."

"Will it hurt?" Oracus asked fearfully.

"Yes, considerably," Shurgda replied. She gathered a different bowl from the shelf and ground its contents with her pestle before adding some pale yellow liquid from a separate container. The mixture hissed and frothed.

"Drink this," she urged, thrusting the bowl into Oracus's

hands.

Oracus wrinkled his nose. "Drink it?"

"It will save your life."

Oracus settled himself and reluctantly tipped the gloopy contents of the bowl into his mouth. It tasted bad, like nothing he had drank before. He swallowed and a pleasant warmth in his throat was followed by an horrific burning in every nerve of his body. He screamed and saw the apologetic look on Shurgda's face. The agony was worse than anything he'd ever felt before, but it refused to leave him. His body tensed and his eyes rolled to the back of his head. Was he dying? Had he been deceived by the Ulatoris? After everything he had survived, was he going to be tortured to death by an Ulatori woman he had foolishly trusted to heal him? The pain heightened and Oracus wailed louder, desperate for relief, but for what seemed like hours it continued to ravage his body.

Finally, when his yelling became loud enough that Shurgda had covered her ears, the pain eased and Oracus panted heavily, exhausted.

"I am sorry," he heard Shurgda say. "The worst of it is over. You should try and get some sleep."

Oracus watched her leave the hut and he stared into the rafters above him, his body still twitching and tingling from its excruciating ordeal. He thought about Bandor, whose mind he still couldn't pinpoint, and hoped he was okay. He'd have tried to search for him if he wasn't so spent. He wondered how the next few days would unravel; whether he would live and escape from Valaroth, or die alone in the hut. Either way, he couldn't shake the thought that his life had turned into a nightmare since that fateful night in the Raspian Forest when he'd become a Rider.

Three

Refugees From Tallarin

The attack on Alvoria would certainly have been a flicker of reality for Jowra, Garrin thought. But its security had been so meagre that he was sure Jowra hadn't seen it as a priority for protection, even if Zarad and Mammat had eventually attempted to save it. Nevertheless, Afarra would take any victory it could; it was a morale boost for the people because it made Jowra appear vulnerable. From the tales Garrin constantly heard, Jowra would prevail no matter how many men opposed him, such was his power. But these days, Garrin questioned why he would have an army at all if his power was as great as the rumours suggested. You would expect a King with immense might and a lack of trust to invade and protect cities single-handedly. Yet, he did not. It seemed he needed his army, and that was enough to give Garrin and his comrades hope.

That being said, the King's army *had* brought about the defeat of Tallarin, even without him. And because of that victory, Afarra was now the only force opposing the King. Half his army had been destroyed in the attack, which gave Garrin a jot of optimism, but the Riders under his command had survived, so the outcome of it all was ultimately worse for the rebellion.

What was more, four Riders had been defending Tallarin, and nobody knew if they were alive. If any of them were dead, then victory for the rebellion would be far less likely. One of the Riders had been Oracus, Garrin's best friend, and since hearing news of the invasion, he'd been hoping Oracus was okay.

Garrin strode out the palace doors and headed towards the training area where Torvanon and Horvos were watching the sparring soldiers. The autumn air was cool, but the morning sun still cast an elegant orange glow over the city. It was the perfect sparring weather for those soldiers preparing to attack Afarra's next target – Fervia.

Shouting men, the clanging of weaponry and the thumping of arrows striking padded targets was what Garrin heard first. It sounded like he'd stepped right onto a battlefield.

"Garrin!" Torvanon bellowed when he spotted Garrin's approach. Torvanon wore his golden armour and carried a huge axe at his waist. His red beard was as bushy as ever and he'd tied his hair back into a ponytail. Stood beside him, Horvos wore the silver armour he never seemed to be without, and his grey beard was as wild as Torvanon's.

"Torvanon, Horvos," Garrin responded with a respectful bow.

"Are you here to train?" Torvanon asked him. "Because there's a group of soldiers over there who are lacking cohesion. Maybe fighting a Rider will help them."

"I'm actually here for your permission," Garrin replied. "I want to travel to Tallarin."

Torvanon rounded on him and frowned. "I can't allow

that," he objected quickly. "I need you for the attack on Fervia."

"I could ride Aquila there and be back in time to join the attack."

"And what if you didn't make it back?" Torvanon asked, shaking his head. "If you died then I wouldn't forgive myself, and your assistance in Fervia is vital to our success."

"But I need to be sure Oracus is alright," Garrin argued. "What if they've captured him or killed him?"

"If he's imprisoned, he'll free himself – he's a Rider. And if he's dead, there's nothing you can do for him now anyway. He knew the risks before he left."

"But I worry he wasn't ready. He didn't even know what his power was before he went. How would he fair in a battle against the King's Riders?"

"Garrin, listen to me," Torvanon said. "I regretted letting Oracus leave the moment he stepped into the Raspian Forest, so I certainly won't make the same mistake with you. But I assure you that Oracus is fine. The survivors from Tallarin will reach us any day now, and you will see him then."

"And what if he doesn't arrive here with the rest of them?"

Torvanon put a hand on Garrin's shoulder. "Go back to your quarters and rest while you can," he advised. "I won't let you fly south, so I need you to be ready for when we march east to Fervia."

The day passed by with Garrin lying against Aquila's ribs on the stone floor of their quarters. He was anxious and fidgety for most of it, so he distracted himself from his thoughts by throwing a small stone around the room with his mind, making it clang loudly on the walls and floor. The room was one of the largest in the palace, big enough to accommodate both him and Aquila, and it had a huge opening in the wall that allowed Aquila to swoop in and out at her leisure.

When the day was getting late and Garrin was growing bored of his isolation, the distant bellow of a horn sounded and he jumped up, losing his focus on the stone and letting it fall to the ground. *"They're here,"* he said, turning to Aquila and then mounting her back. *"Take us to the drawbridge."*

The bells above the palace chimed as Aquila took off, and Garrin could see soldiers running hurriedly through the streets nearest the palace. Garrin's long blonde hair flowed wildly as Aquila climbed towards the blue sky, and his heart hammered excitedly in his chest. Afarra was a vast city, but looking down from such a height he could see all the buildings like stones on a gravel footpath.

When they completed their ascent, Garrin could see the moat and wall that surrounded the city. To the west, both ends of the moat fell into the ocean, but to the east, archers were gathering on the ramparts and aiming their bows across the grassy plains ahead.

Aquila dived on Garrin's order and the two came to a hover above the drawbridge. Aquila forced her senses onto Garrin, and his eyes narrowed on four-hundred people approaching from where the grass met the Raspian Forest in the distance. Using Aquila's vision, Garrin could see the incoming force as if they were only a few feet from him. The entire group was bloodied and filthy, with most of them women or children. Many looked starved, like they hadn't eaten a good meal for many days, and Garrin wasn't sure if the walk across the plains might be enough to finish some of them off. As the crowd trudged slowly across the grass, Garrin scoured the group for Oracus, but his friend wasn't with them. He could see Kivali though, and it was her who led the group with her Jaguar Lavorian, Onca.

"Lower the bridge!" Garrin ordered the guards as he and Aquila landed beside the portcullis. "They're from Tallarin."

The guards looked at each other, unsure whether to respect Garrin's command.

"Do as he asks," Torvanon's voice boomed from behind Garrin. He approached them with a look of concern on his face. "And let's hope that isn't their only party."

"I can see Kivali with them, but not Oracus," Garrin said worriedly.

"Then at least we know one Rider is alive and well," Torvanon said. The broad-chested leader then directed more orders at the guards. When the drawbridge landed, a score of soldiers marched onto the grasslands to meet the people from Tallarin and aid the weakest.

Before long, the group reached the lowered drawbridge and were taken into inspection houses by medics. Most of the suffering was through thirst and hunger, but some had walked to exhaustion and needed further care. An elderly man was carried on a stretcher by two guards, while a young girl had ridden Onca's back for the final stint.

"More groups should be following us in the coming days," Kivali advised Torvanon as she stepped under the portcullis behind her people. "There were eleven parties all told."

"You split up?" Torvanon asked.

"We thought smaller groups would draw less attention,"

she said, sighing and drinking from a flask a guard had given her. "It's lucky we had the tunnels in the mountains to escape through, otherwise we'd have no groups at all."

Garrin stepped in front of Kivali as she reached Torvanon. "Is Oracus alive?" he questioned her hopefully.

Kivali turned to him, her usually vibrant eyes dull and empty in a face so thin and gaunt. "He hasn't been seen since the battle."

"You mean he's dead?" Garrin said fearfully.

"I have no idea," she returned. She faced Torvanon then and offered him a steely gaze. "We need to meet in your council room," she stated. "There are important matters we must address."

"It would be better if you rested first, Kivali," Torvanon suggested. "The ordeal has exhausted you."

"I can rest after. This is urgent."

Torvanon bowed his head and ushered Garrin and Kivali to follow him. They walked in silence through the city streets and proceeded to the palace entrance. When they had passed through the halls inside and reached the council room, it was waiting for them as stifling as ever. Already, the single lamp had been lit, and Horvos sat waiting for them.

"Is Jowra's army still large enough to defeat us here in Afarra?" Horvos asked when they'd barely stepped foot in the room.

The scrape of chairs came next as the three of them took to their seats around Horvos.

"He suffered thousands of casualties, for sure. But I doubt every one of his soldiers were there. He'll have more waiting elsewhere."

"Agreed," Torvanon said glumly. "It may take him

several months, but I expect Jowra to strike us as soon as he can. He'll know we're weak."

"Our defences are well prepared for any attacks though," Horvos stated. "He might regret it when the time comes."

"Not if he joins the fight himself," Torvanon disputed. He turned to Kivali. "How many men will arrive from Tallarin?"

"If every group makes it, about six-thousand. But only a quarter of those are soldiers."

"And how many Riders will accompany them?"

"Only Dyma escaped with me," Kivali said.

"Only two of you?" Horvos cried. "Are you saying Oracus and Wilos are dead?"

"Neither escaped through the tunnels," Kivali said. "That is all I know."

"My goodness," Horvos uttered, shaking his head. "It's a catastrophe."

"I would advise you to reconsider your defences, Torvanon," Kivali recommended.

"Do you think we under-estimate our enemy?" Horvos asked irritably. "We know what we're up against."

"We thought we knew what to expect too, but Tallarin has fallen," Kivali said.

"We have already altered our strategy, don't worry," Torvanon said. "Sitting back and defending our city like Catania did with Tallarin will get us nowhere."

"So you're going to attack Jowra first?" Kivali said with a laugh. "That's ridiculous."

"We already have attacked him. We destroyed Alvoria only a few weeks ago," Torvanon explained. "And we're going to invade Fervia next."

"But when I was last here, you agreed not to provoke

Jowra."

"Circumstances change," Torvanon stated. "Are you not happy that we're fighting for Pharia's survival?"

"Not if your attack on Alvoria was the reason Jowra sent his army to Tallarin!" Kivali shouted angrily.

"We are doing what is right for this land," Torvanon responded.

"You are only doing what is best for your city," Kivali retaliated. "Casualties elsewhere obviously aren't important to you. Hundreds died at the battle in Tallarin and some of them were my closest friends: Princess Catania, Shio, Wilos, Edinuc. None of them got out alive."

"I'm sorry for your losses, Kivali. But none of their deaths are my fault," Torvanon answered.

"And I suppose it wasn't your fault either that Princess Catania was killed by Oracus? The man you led us to believe was trusthworthy."

"What?" Garrin blurted out. "Oracus wouldn't do that."

"He cut Alticon's throat and shot an arrow through Catania's heart," Kivali snapped.

"Jowra's men killed Oracus's father. He wouldn't fight for them," Garrin reasoned.

"It turns out Oracus's grandfather is King Jowra himself," Kivali retorted. "They are one of a kind!"

Garrin's mouth dropped open. "You must have made a mistake."

"There is no mistake. He slaughtered our leader," Kivali said angrily. "And he's a Vassath Rider like his grandfather."

"A Vassath too?" Horvos said. "If this is true… If Jowra and Oracus have united… Well, I dread to think how soon we'll meet our end."

Torvanon stroked his beard, concern etched on his face like Garrin had never seen before. "We must stick to the plan," he said simply. "That is all we can do. We mustn't give up now." He pushed back his chair and stood. "Garrin, I need you and Aquila to scout Fervia so we know what to expect when we arrive. Kivali, rest until tomorrow. When you're ready, I want you to round up any men from Tallarin who are still willing to fight. We need as many fighters as possible for what comes next. Fervia will fall, but we need to be ready for any retaliation."

FOUR

Sarvon

It had taken eight days of healing before Oracus's body would allow him to stand, and a further twelve until he could walk without assistance. The medicine to cure his broken body had thankfully worked, but the almost endless pain had been unforgiving. Shurgda had been Oracus's only company throughout the ordeal too. Sarvon, nor any other Ulatoris, had entered the hut to check on his progress, not that Oracus would have expected them to, so he soon felt lonely. It didn't help that his connection with Bandor was still severed either, for it would have been nice to have the Lion in his mind. Oracus often asked Shurgda if he could see the Lavorian, but the answer was always no.

The twentieth day was when Oracus decided to explore. He needed to see something other than the dark wooden innards of the hut he hadn't left since his arrival. He was sure he wouldn't be allowed to leave, so he waited for Shurgda to depart before staggering unsteadily across the room. He pushed open the flimsy door and found himself blinded by the bright daylight he hadn't seen for so long. It took a moment for his eyes to adjust, but soon he could see dozens of Ulatoris who had turned to look at him. Oracus doubted they often saw other races in their village, and it was clear the sight of him angered them. They were all muscular and intimidating, both the men and women, and many had tattoos or piercings. Although none were as tall and broad as Sarvon, they still made Oracus feel tiny.

Stood in the doorway of Shurgda's hut, Oracus was on the edge of the icy village square, which was surrounded by other wooden huts with doors twice as large as those in Thessley. Above the huts were the snowy tops of the Black Forest's trees that reached high towards the grey, wintry sky, their presence magnificent but frightening. In the centre of the square was the metal structure Oracus had been bound to those many days ago, untouched and slick with ice. He briefly wondered how many Humans had been killed whilst hanging from it, but then forced the thought away.

Oracus was barefoot on the snow and wore only a thin robe to protect his dignity. He shivered violently but advanced nevertheless, keen not to show weakness to the Ulatoris nearby. The ground crunched underfoot as he limped across the square, and soon his toes were blue with cold. He made a beeline for the nearest Ulatori, whose thick brows were furrowed into a scowl.

"Erm… hello. Do you know where Sarvon is?" he asked apprehensively, looking up at the huge Ulatori.

The Ulatori growled, clearly unhappy that Oracus had dared speak to him. The other Ulatoris nearby also hissed their displeasure.

Oracus backed away as the Ulatori rounded on him, and he jumped when a large hand grasped his shoulder from behind. He turned and found himself faced by an elderly Ulatori with a tangled white beard and a less fearsome expression.

"You should not be out here," he said hoarsely. "It is dangerous."

"I needed some air," Oracus said timidly, suddenly very aware of how vulnerable he was. He tried to pull out of the Ulatori's grasp, but his grip was too strong.

"Come with me," the Ulatori stated, and pressing on Oracus's shoulder, he forced him to move.

Oracus was led away from the glaring eyes in the square. He limped alongside the old Ulatori as quickly as he could, but his legs weren't yet strong enough and he stumbled several times.

"You must not walk by yourself in this village," the Ulatori explained to Oracus when they were between huts and out of sight. "Many of my race want you dead."

Oracus merely nodded his head.

"Sarvon's decision to let you live has caused him difficulty with some of the more rebellious villagers."

"Don't they trust him?" Oracus asked quietly.

The Ulatori looked at Oracus, his yellow eyes reading him carefully. "No, some of them do not."

"But they could have killed me while I was healing in Shurgda's hut," Oracus said.

"They would not go to such lengths to disobey Sarvon," the Ulatori advised. "But with you outside and unprotected, they could be tempted."

"Sorry, I didn't realise," Oracus muttered.

They stopped at a grand, stone building with marvellous patterns carved into its face. Oracus was sure it was Sarvon's abode, for the building was far superior to any of the wooden others surrounding it.

"My name is Olf," the Ulatori said as he directed Oracus

through the stone door.

"I'm Oracus," Oracus replied with a friendly smile.

The building's internals were much less grandiose than the outside had led Oracus to expect. It was one large room, mostly grey other than the wooden rafters in the roof-space. There were no windows to offer light, only a crackling fire in the fireplace that glowed orange and filled the room with scent of burning wood. In the centre of the room was a square stone table, and seated at the table was Sarvon, with a black fur coat flowing from his broad shoulders to the floor, and an ugly silver crown sat on his bald, tattooed head. At Olf and Oracus's arrival, he didn't raise his eyes from an enormous axe lying on the table.

"You have not fully recovered, Rider. Shurgda has not permitted you to leave her care." He still didn't look up, but he placed his hands on the table and interlaced his fingers.

"I'm a lot better, Sir," Oracus replied politely, glad to be out of the cold and stood near the warm fire.

"Well enough to begin your training?" Sarvon enquired.

"I think so," Oracus said.

"But you can hardly walk," Sarvon observed, finally lifting his head to look at Oracus. He slammed his fists onto the table and made Oracus jump. "How do you expect to survive your training like this?"

Oracus's words caught in his mouth and he failed to reply.

"Take him back to Shurgda, Olf," Sarvon ordered. He ran his fingers along the shaft of his axe and then waved his hand dismissively. "My patience is already wearing thin with this Human."

"I might still be in pain but I'm ready to train!" Oracus

declared, finding his voice and using it more forcefully than he'd intended. "And I'm not just a Human, I'm a Rider too."

Sarvon stood slowly and Oracus expected to receive admonishment. But instead, a wry smile came to the Ulatori's lips. "Very well." He turned to Olf. "Leave us to be alone, my friend."

Olf bowed respectfully and exited, allowing a frigid gust of wind to sneak in and make Oracus shiver.

"Sit," Sarvon ordered, pointing at a chair opposite him.

Oracus obliged and settled at the table, happy to take the weight off his legs.

"What do you think makes a Rider?" Sarvon asked him, his voice now much calmer than when he spoke in front of his villagers.

The simple question threw Oracus, "Erm… I don't know."

"A Rider is a leader with incredible power *and* control," Sarvon answered for him. "Jowra and Gravaz kill to be powerful but they do not know how to control themselves." Sarvon's lip curled momentarily. "They are not worthy of being Riders or rulers of this land."

Oracus nodded in agreement.

"I would have killed you had I been like them," Sarvon stated.

"I'm surprised you didn't," Oracus admitted.

"Your life was almost ended because other Ulatoris here wanted me to end it," Sarvon said. "But I found control and did what I believe is right."

"You think it's right to keep me alive despite what your people think?" Oracus asked.

"As a Rider, you should be welcomed to Valaroth,"

Sarvon answered. "Even if you are of another race."

"Why do the other Ulatoris think differently?"

"Because they have good reason to."

"I haven't done anything wrong though," Oracus confuted.

"It is not you who created this mistrust we feel, it comes from others in your race." Sarvon explained. "But I think you can change that."

"How?" Oracus asked with an uncertain frown.

"By doing what you agreed to do, and by proving your allegiance to Valaroth."

"I need to find Gravaz and bring him here," Oracus said, repeating what Sarvon himself had said when Oracus was tied up.

Sarvon nodded. "Ulatoris believe your race to be power-hungry and selfish. Aiding us to punish Gravaz for his treachery would force them to reconsider their views."

"But why keep me here?" Oracus asked. "Just send me to get Gravaz now."

Sarvon raised his eyebrows and smiled. "We both know you would leave and never come back. But if you live and train here under my supervision, then I hope you will come to understand that keeping to our agreement is beneficial for you as well as us." Sarvon adjusted the crown on his head. "And if you embrace our culture while you reside here, it will hopefully help the Ulatoris realise that not all Humans need to die."

"But if I fail then your people will hate Humans all the more." Oracus said with a shake of his head. He felt it was unfair that the Ulatoris' trust of Humans was placed entirely on his shoulders.

Sarvon shrugged. "Since Jowra left Valaroth many years

ago, no other race has been allowed access here," he said. "Consider yourself fortunate to be alive, and try not to feel hard done to."

"What did Jowra do here that was so bad?"

"I will not discuss that with you just yet," Sarvon said. "And it would be wise of you to refrain from asking another Ulatori that same question."

"Sure," Oracus accepted, somewhat disappointedly.

Sarvon stood then and pulled his axe from the table. "Would you like to see your Lavorian?" he asked.

Forgetting about the pain in his legs, Oracus jumped up excitedly and almost fell over. "Yes!" he said. "Is he okay?"

"He is fine," Sarvon answered. He opened the door and another cold draught swept through the room. The flames of the fire flickered unhappily. "A forewarning before we step outside, Human: when we are near other Ulatoris, I will be far less friendly. It would make them uneasy otherwise."

Together, they stepped out of Sarvon's abode and started along the snowy path outside. Oracus still wore only his cotton robe, and his bare feet felt even colder after adapting to the warmth of the fire.

They walked slowly between Valaroth's buildings given Oracus's injuries, and Oracus attracted sneers from the Ulatoris they passed. Sarvon didn't speak or discourage the misanthropists, he only guided Oracus in silence.

Beyond the buildings, they encountered a long but narrow fenced area with a gate. Inside the fencing were dozens of fortified cages large enough to contain some bizarre animals Oracus did not recognise. Their grunting was loud and unpleasant, as was their smell, and Oracus scrunched his nose at the odour. The animals looked like wild pigs, just larger and more ferocious, and their eyes were as black as their matted hair. Each pig had a pair of destructive tusks protruding from both their top and bottom jaws, and they scuffed their trotters against the floor to show their frustration at being confined. At the sight of Oracus and Sarvon, the creatures began to squeal, and they smashed aggressively at the insides of their cages.

Oracus flinched and took a step backwards. "What are they?" he asked Sarvon, horrified.

"Chagris," Sarvon answered.

"Are they dangerous?"

"Not to the Ulatoris," Sarvon said. "But they can smell your unfamiliar flesh. You are lucky you did not encounter any Chagris in the forest when you arrived here. They hunt in packs and you would have been killed and eaten in mere minutes."

They followed the aisle of cages, Oracus with far more uncertainty than his Ulatori guide, until Sarvon stopped. He pointed at the last cage on their right.

"Bandor!" Oracus exclaimed.

The Lavorian looked defeated in his cage, but the sight of Oracus made his eyes light up. "I hope you're here to let me out," he said.

Oracus looked at Sarvon who nodded and unlocked the door of the cage. Bandor exited and stretched his legs, before rubbing his head affectionately against Oracus's side.

"Why can't I connect with his mind?" Oracus asked Sarvon as he ran his fingers through the Lion's mane.

"Shurgda fed you a potion that disrupts your bond," he replied. "I need to be sure that you and your Lavorian are trustworthy before you can join minds again."

Oracus was unhappy with Sarvon's confession, but seeing Bandor for the first time in weeks was what mattered to him right now. He turned his attention back to his Lavorian. "Have you been alright?"

"I'm fine," Bandor said. "I was worried about you though. I heard your screams on the first day we were here."

"I'm okay now," Oracus assured. "Have you been in that cage for all the time we've been here?"

"They've not let me out once!" Bandor exclaimed. He looked around at the other cages. "And these creatures are foul!"

Oracus rounded on Sarvon. "We'll both be staying in Shurgda's hut together from now on, right?"

"The arrangements will remain as they are for the foreseeable future, Rider," Sarvon denied.

"But why?" Oracus probed with irritation.

"Because my people will feel uneasy if your Lavorian is out his cage," Sarvon answered.

Oracus felt inclined to argue with Sarvon, but his fear of provoking the Ulatori stopped him.

"I suggest you get back in your cage, Lavorian," Sarvon went on. "Your Rider's training will begin in the coming days and he is yet to take Shurgda's potions for today. If he doesn't rest and heal then he may not survive what I have planned for him."

Oracus wrapped his arms around Bandor's neck and hugged him goodbye. "See you soon," he said sadly.

Sarvon then locked Bandor inside the cage and led Oracus back through the gate and towards the centre of Valaroth. While they walked, Oracus couldn't help wondering how long and tough his time in Valaroth would be. All that was keeping him from desperation was the thought of Garrin and Torvanon fronting the rebellion, and the hope that Kivali had escaped Tallarin and found refuge somewhere safe.

FIVE

Alu'reath

As he had anticipated, Oracus found the following days difficult. While Bandor was locked in his cage, Oracus was kept within the wooden walls of Shurgda's hut, with no natural light or fresh air besides what crept through the crack of the door. The darkness and overwhelming scent of herbal medicines exhausted him, and he regularly fell into an agitated sleep.

Shurgda continued to heal his body, rubbing some concoctions into his skin and forcing others down his throat. Throughout it all, he experienced a lot of pain, but he was grateful to the Ulatori because he felt much stronger than he had on his arrival to Valaroth. His legs were steadier now and he could walk and stand freely without much soreness in his muscles. And the wounds that had covered his body before were now gone except for a bit of scarring.

The weather on the day Oracus's training began was blizzardous. Sleet lashed ferociously from the sky and hammered against the roofs of Valaroth's huts, while the wind billowed snow in every direction. Oracus wondered if the weather might force Sarvon to postpone his training, but apparently the Ulatoris are quite used to sleet and biting winds, and they complete their duties as if it was any other day.

It came as a relief for Oracus when Sarvon led him out of Valaroth and into the forest, for the sleet was sharp against his sensitive skin until the trees sheltered him. But with a respite from the weather came a darkness in the forest that only reminded him of the endless painful days he had spent in Shurgda's hut. This forest wasn't warm and peaceful like the Raspian Forest up north, it was cold and eerily silent, like the creatures here knew not to draw attention to themselves.

Oracus found himself scanning the forest around him, but such was the darkness, he could see nothing except Sarvon's huge silhouette carving a path through the undergrowth in front of him. He could hear nothing either besides the crunch of dead leaves and twigs underfoot, and the patter of sleet on the canopy high overhead. It was a vulnerable place to be, and Oracus was putting his faith in Sarvon to keep him safe.

Oracus wore his armour and footwear from Tallarin. His leather boots were saturated from the snow and the sapphire blue metal of his chestplate and gauntlets did very little to stave off the cold. He wished there was something warmer to wear, but all other clothing in the village belonged to Ulatoris, and everything was far too big for him. Even the children were much broader across the shoulders, and Sarvon wasn't willing to have anything made for him.

After several long minutes walking in silence, the denseness of the trees began to ease, and lines of light began to break through the forest ceiling. Here, Sarvon picked up his pace and Oracus was forced to jog to keep up.

"Where are we going?" Oracus asked, breathing heavily.

"You will know soon enough," Sarvon responded. "We are almost there."

Oracus groaned but kept speed with Sarvon's long strides until the Ulatori came to a halt. Oracus almost walked into the back of him he'd stopped so suddenly, but when the Ulatori stepped aside, Oracus let out a gasp of amazement.

They had entered a clearing occupied by a tree grander than any Oracus had seen before. From where he stood, it appeared thrice the height of any other tree around it, and the girth of its trunk was beyond comparison. The beauty of the tree's pink blossom was matched only by the white light that emanated from the bark, leaving a magical glow to cascade around the otherwise dark clearing. Many of the tree's topmost roots were scattered over the uneven ground, leaving small canyons that were full of brittle brown leaves.

"It's beautiful," Oracus stated, eagerly eyeing the tree.

"It is Iniril," Sarvon replied. "The tree of knowing."

"What does it do?" Oracus asked.

"Its purpose is to enlighten. The Ulatoris travel here to pray, and in return, Iniril shares its knowledge and power," Sarvon explained. He knelt and ran a colossal, but delicate, hand along a thick root that had partially surfaced. "You can feel its presence; its voice whispers."

Oracus looked at several roots around him. They had caused the ground to dip in places, and brittle brown leaves had gathered in piles. At Sarvon's touch, Oracus had felt the ground tremble.

"Iniril will enter your mind and uncover both your

potential and your destiny," Sarvon said.

"Can it tell me my future?" Oracus quizzed.

"No, Rider. It will only offer you a chance to follow the right path," Sarvon said. "You may pray if you wish."

Oracus considered the choice but refused. "I can't."

"Why not?" Sarvon enquired.

"Because I don't feel like I've earned the right to pray to something your race considers holy," Oracus stated.

"I will not be offended if you do."

Oracus shook his head, "Maybe another time."

"Very well," Sarvon responded, unfazed. He held the root tighter and closed his eyes. For several seconds, the ground trembled some more.

"Why have you brought me here?" Oracus asked when Sarvon released the root and stood. "I thought we were starting my training."

"You are single-minded, Rider. I will teach you to fight of course, but that is not the only way to train."

"What do you mean?"

"Speaking with Iniril is training, learning the ways of the Ulatoris is training, becoming knowledgeable, courageous and decisive is training." Sarvon spoke frankly. "Killing with a weapon is for the weak and the dumb. Knowing when not to draw a weapon is a skill everyone should possess, but very few attempt to learn."

Oracus remembered Sarvon's words back when he was to be killed in Valaroth's square and he spoke them aloud, "A race so weak it fights and destroys anything it can in an attempt to prove its power."

"Well remembered," Sarvon praised. His lips curled into a smile. "Words are far wiser."

"So what will you have me doing today?" Oracus

probed.

"My only plan was to introduce you to Iniril," Sarvon said. "That is until we were accompanied on our journey here."

"Accompanied?" Oracus asked, looking nervously over his shoulder at the wall of trees behind him.

"Your observation is poor, Rider," Sarvon criticised. "We were followed here by a wild Narborg."

"A Narborg?"

Sarvon didn't explain. Instead, he cupped his hands over his mouth and let out a shriek that made Oracus jump. As soon as Sarvon uncovered his mouth, a mimicked cry replied from just within the treeline, and then a monstrous beast came charging into the clearing. It stopped a yard short of them and Oracus cried out in fear and clung to Sarvon's arm. The Narborg was impressive, if terrifying. Standing like a wolf but on six legs, it was as tall as Oracus and covered in small spines. It was the same jet black as the forest but for its green eyes, and Oracus realised its incredible camouflage was why he hadn't spotted it before.

"Your fear is riling her, Rider," Sarvon said. "Your calmness will prompt hers."

"Calmness?" Oracus whimpered. He took a step behind Sarvon. "It wants to kill us!"

"And she will try to kill us if you do not face her!" Sarvon exclaimed.

The Narborg growled menacingly and the lips of its snout curled back to uncover a set of dagger-like teeth.

"But–"

"Release your fear, Rider," Sarvon demanded. "Now!"

Although his instincts were to run, Oracus obeyed Sarvon and slowly stood out from behind the Ulatori. The

Narborg's spines quivered and lowered at the sight of Oracus's face. Its pupils dilated as its aggression appeared to ease.

"Now place a hand upon her snout," Sarvon advised.

Oracus took a step forward and raised his hand, keeping his eyes firmly on the beast's. The moment reminded him so vividly of his introduction to Bandor; the dark forest, the apprehension, even the beautiful glow of Iniril was similar to that of the Orbular from which Bandor was born. The memory erased all Oracus's worries and his fingers met the Narborg's surprisingly wet nose. The Narborg closed its eyes and its spines quivered with pleasure this time. It pressed against Oracus's palm, and Oracus scratched under its chin. Then two previously hidden wings fell from its sides and wafted in the cold, breezy air.

"She likes you," Sarvon said.

"And I like her," Oracus replied, rubbing the Narborg's neck and laughing.

"There are many creatures in this forest, Rider," Sarvon said. "To survive here you must learn to understand them. A Narborg will feel threatened by your fear, but other beasts may not be so accepting of your courage."

"What other creatures are there?" Oracus asked.

"You will come to recognise them soon enough."

"Your Lavorian is a Narborg, isn't it?" Oracus said. The Lavorian he had seen in Valaroth when he first arrived resembled this creature.

"Yes," Sarvon replied. "Her name is Tarnu."

"How long have you been a Rider?" Oracus probed curiously.

"Tens of years."

"And what is your power?"

Sarvon looked suspiciously at Oracus. "I would prefer to keep that a secret for today. Come, it is time we returned to Valaroth."

Sarvon placed a hand on the Narborg's crown, and without a sound, it trotted back into the tree's depths.

"She will always remember your scent, Rider," Sarvon stated as he began to walk. "She will never forget you."

Oracus nodded and glanced back at Iniril's glow. He wondered what else in the forest would surprise him before he was due to leave. In the short time he'd been in Valaroth and the Black Forest, he had already witnessed such fascinating creatures and wildlife. Perhaps life here wasn't to be as harsh as he'd expected. Maybe, he thought, life with the Ulatoris suited him more than it did elsewhere.

*

The following evening arrived and Oracus regretted his optimism. Sarvon, Iniril and the Narborg had given him false hope that Valaroth wasn't actually full of savages. Unfortunately, it was.

Snow had fallen heavily throughout the night and following day, and a fresh chill was hanging over Valaroth. Being from the north, Oracus had never known anything other than sunshine and warm rain, so the untouched snow by the sides of the paths he found fascinating, and he wondered how it had been formed in the sky.

The sun was descending behind the forest's dark trees, and Oracus was stood in Valaroth's war circle. He wore no armour, only the rags issued to him by the Ulatoris on his arrival to the village. He was cold and shivering in the snow, and wondering how he'd found himself in such a predicament.

The war circle was surrounded by Valaroth's people. On each night of the month when the moon was fullest, the Ulatoris would host an event called Alu'reath. Alu'reath had once been used to maintain the hierarchy of the Ulatori army, should they ever find themselves in a war. The better fighters would achieve higher ranks, and permission would be granted for them to ride Chagris and Narborgs into battle. Alu'reath now was merely for the entertainment of the villagers. Several one-on-one fights would take place, with the combatants only allowed to use their fists, and the winner of each fight would move on to fight someone else. In the end, the winner would gain a measure of power within Valaroth, and a Chagri to ride on would be gifted to them as a prize. Oracus knew all this because of Olf. The elderly Ulatori had been helpful since Sarvon's decision to include Oracus in the tournament, but that didn't stop Oracus fearing he might get killed.

So in the war circle he was, facing an Ulatori woman called Mechuce, and armed with only his clenched fists. Mechuce was muscular and frightening, with white tribal paints on her skin that interlinked with her tattoos. She wore almost no clothes, which in itself disconcerted Oracus. In Valaroth, such exposure didn't seem unusual, but Oracus couldn't help imagining the outrage of the villagers in Thessley had he been in the same situation with a lady there.

The proximity of the spectators intimidated Oracus as much as fighting Mechuce. They were tightly packed and about five Ulatoris deep, and they all swayed and chanted as they waited for the fight to begin. Some of the spectators were sat on the shoulders of others to get a better view, and some had even climbed onto the roofs of the huts so they could watch and laugh as the weak Human got beaten to a pulp.

A loud horn blared from somewhere outside the war circle and the crowd jeered and growled. Mechuce was quick to approach Oracus, but he dodged her advance just as Olf had wisely advised him. Mechuce immediately came after him again and threw a fist, but Oracus was agile enough to avoid her a second time.

"I will tear the flesh from your bones!" she yelled in frustration.

Oracus evaded Mechuce's attacks for as long as he could, but with every miss, the crowd seemed to close in. Soon, Oracus felt like he had nowhere left to run, and Mechuce eventually seized him. She threw him to the ground like a doll and sat triumphantly upon his chest. The crowd bellowed its approval as she held her hands aloft, and then she brought them down onto Oracus's face. The pain and blood came together in an instant, and he knew then that he'd lost, it had taken less than a minute.

Mechuce hit him several more times until the numbness came and the Ulatoris celebrated. Then the warmth of the blood became heavy in his eyes and he drifted inevitably into unconsciousness.

SIX

Ulatori Culture

King Xarmoud lay alone in his quarters, pondering his persistent thoughts of war. One-hundred Riders had fallen to the swords of the Fizorachis; the race in black. They had travelled from a distant homeland to take Pharia for their own and turn it into a land of darkness. Their race was strong and agile, and their skill with a sword remarkable, turning even the most courageous of Xarmoud's soldiers into whimpering cowards.

Xarmoud knew he must stop them. The descent of this race from the north brought with it dark clouds, cold rain and terrible thunderstorms, and it struck fear into the hearts of innocents. Talk was of the Fizorachis' leader, Vlaem, whose name had spread across Pharia like fire through a dry forest. Vlaem rode upon an armoured creature that wasn't dissimilar to a Lavorian, and with black armour and three raging red eyes, it was as terrifying as it was large. If any of Xarmoud's men avoided the lesser Fizorachis, they wouldn't escape Vlaem and his monster. And neither would the innocents, even if they were on their knees in surrender.

Xarmoud had dreamt of the past, a skill inherited from

his mother. And in those dreams, he had heard his ancestors speak of these evil Fizorachis. The Humans had been victorious once before, but the race in black had almost taken Pharia. The army of Xarmoud's forefathers had been depleted to only several-hundred, and thousands of women and children had been murdered while their fine cities were reduced to dust. But Xarmoud's ancestors had somehow earned victory in that war, and now it was his turn to send the invaders back to the land from which they came.

Xarmoud rose to his feet and strode across the marble floor to where his royal armour hung on the wall; golden and majestic. He donned the armour, then grabbed his sword and necklace from the dresser, both encrusted with green emeralds that brought exceptional power to their holder. But even with the Emerald Pairing, Xarmoud was vulnerable. With the vast armies that Vlaem brought with him, there was every chance Xarmoud would die. Nevertheless, he had a duty to his people. He was the only Rider left, and the only one powerful enough to bring an end to the invasion.

*

Oracus opened his eyes and saw the familiar wooden rafters above him. He was lying in Shurgda's hut, with the strong scent of herbs and medicine deep in his nostrils. His first thought was to connect to Bandor's mind and discuss his dream about King Xarmoud, but he quickly remembered their bond had been severed by Shurgda's potions.

"Shurgda," Oracus said as he rolled onto his side.

"Ahh, you are awake," she replied. She put down the bowl she was holding and gave him a curious look.

"What happened?" he asked. "Why does my face hurt?"

"You do not remember?"

"No."

"You were almost killed in Alu'reath," Shurgda explained. "Mechuce got quite an applause from the other villagers."

Her words provoked the memories to come flooding back and Oracus groaned.

"I am beginning to lose count of how many times I have saved your life," Shurgda said, her gentle voice carrying sarcasm. "You have slept for three full days."

"Have I scarred?"

"I have healed you the best I can," Shurgda replied. "But there is a little scarring, yes. You are starting to look like a war hero."

"I feel more like a loser than a hero," Oracus answered honestly.

A gentle knock came to the door and it swung inwards. With a draught of cold air, Olf stepped in with flecks of snow in his grey beard.

"The Human returns to us!" he stated when he saw Oracus was awake. "You took quite a beating. The Ulatoris are calling you *Devol Eib*."

"Devol Eib?" Oracus quizzed.

"Weak Human," Olf explained, not mincing his words. "Words spoken from our language."

Oracus groaned again. Being seen as weak by the Ulatoris was the last thing he wanted. He needed them to consider him capable if he was ever going to be allowed to leave and bring Gravaz back to their village.

"Sarvon has asked me to see you," Olf stated. "Should you be awake, which you are, you are to resume training."

"I don't think I can," Oracus rejected.

"That is not your choice," Olf stated. "But do not worry, your training will be with me and it involves neither fists nor blood."

"Then what does it involve?" Oracus asked ominously.

"You will see, come now."

Oracus reluctantly did as he was told and accompanied Olf through the village to the old Ulatori's hut. The moment he stepped foot in the square, mocking cries of *Devol Eib* were shouted at him, and balls of snow were thrown his way. Oracus did his best to ignore them, but was glad when they moved out of range.

Olf's hut was the same as Shurgda's. Its size, structure and rafters were identical, but the shelves in there contained books, not medicines. There was a large bed in one corner and a desk in the other, and a black fur rug on the floor that was wiry between Oracus's toes.

"Can you tell me now what training we're going to be doing?" Oracus asked, looking around the room with interest.

"I will be testing your knowledge," Olf replied, settling down in the chair beside the desk. "So tell me first: what you know about us Ulatoris?"

"Not a lot really," Oracus answered with a shrug.

"You know nothing of our heritage, our ancestry, our culture?"

Oracus shook his head. "Until my village was attacked a few months ago, I didn't know about the rest of Pharia, let alone who lived in the Black Forest."

Olf interlaced his fingers as he studied Oracus. "Take a

seat," he offered.

Oracus sat on the end of Olf's bed. It was so high off the ground that his feet couldn't touch the floor, so he swung them loosely like he used to when he was a child.

"In my seventy years of life I haven't once passed beyond the edges of this forest," Olf said. "And for that reason, I do not know how we are perceived by outsiders. I was hoping maybe you could enlighten me."

"I've been told that the Black Forest is a dangerous place, and that's it," Oracus said. "I never had reason to ask further questions."

"Whoever told you that is right; it is a dangerous place."

Oracus nodded in agreement. He was well aware of the creatures lurking in the trees. "Have any of the villagers here travelled?" he asked.

"Other than Gravaz, no Ulatori has left the forest in fifty years."

"Are you not curious as to what's out there?"

Olf let out a throaty laugh. "This is our home; we want no business with outsiders. It would not benefit our race to be dragged into a war that is not our own." Olf raised his eyebrows and then reached up to one of the shelves beside him. He ran his fingers along the spines of his books. "Books fascinate me," he said.

"I like books too," Oracus said. "But I haven't read much at all since I left my village."

Olf pulled a thin book free of the others and handed it to Oracus. "Take this. It will give you some idea how we perceive you Humans," he said. "Read it when you are bored in Shurgda's hut."

Oracus was horrified to see a dying Human on the cover of the book, but he accepted it and thanked Olf nonetheless.

"I guess being here is difficult for you," Olf spoke on. "A lot of people here hate you."

"It's not easy," Oracus agreed. "But I'm getting used to it."

"Do you wish to leave?"

"I'd like to see my friends again. They probably think I'm dead so it would be nice to show them I'm not."

"You will in time," Olf advised. "But you have a lot to learn before then."

"That's what Sarvon told me," Oracus said. "But I don't think I can be any better than I am now."

"Of course you can," Olf said. "You are a Rider."

"But I've had my powers taken from me," Oracus complained. "I can't improve if I don't have them."

"You have been blinded by your teachers in the past," Olf stated. "Until now, you have only learnt to fight with a sword, like all Humans. Ulatoris are taught to fight with their hands, and only when they have mastered that are they permitted to wield a weapon."

"But how can I practise with my fists when I will be knocked unconscious within seconds by the Ulatori I'm fighting?"

"You would be surprised how quickly you improve when you are beaten bloody every time you lose," Olf advised. "I am sure there are children here who would allow you a fairer fight."

"I can't fight with children!" Oracus exclaimed. "That would be appalling."

"Your race do not fight their children?" Olf asked, dumbstruck.

"No! We would get imprisoned."

"That is unusual. Here, we would not judge you for striking a child. In fact, if you beat a child in a fight, we would return to you your sword and powers."

Oracus frowned unhappily. He wouldn't stoop to such levels to get his powers back. And even if he did, hitting a youngster wouldn't guarantee him victory anyway; the children here were all his size or larger.

"But enough about fighting," Olf said. "You are with me to better understand our culture. Maybe if you learn more about us, you will not act in such a way that will make us hate you."

Oracus listened for hours as Olf explained how the Ulatoris lived. Politeness was weakness, as was laziness, and rule-breaking was punishable by death. The more Oracus took in, the better he understood life in Valaroth. The Ulatoris' culture was far different to his own, yet far simpler. Men, women and children were treated equally, and they all worked together as one. Aside from Sarvon's leadership and the authority gifted to the winners of Alu'reath, there was no obvious hierarchy. Everybody in the village had a role to play, and they completed their tasks with the utmost effort. Hunters would be relied upon for food, cooks for preparing meals, woodsmen for shelter, guards for protection, and Shurgda for healing. And there were many more duties performed by others elsewhere.

For decades, nothing had damaged their unity, not since Gravaz had decamped. But now their togetherness was being tested, for another Human within their ranks was like poison in their veins – another Jowra. Allowing Oracus to live had called Sarvon's judgement into question, and if Sarvon was relieved of his leadership, then Oracus, as Olf explained, was as good as dead.

SEVEN

Sparring To The Death

Over the following days, thousands of Tallarin evacuees followed Kivali and Onca into Afarra in several separate groups; each clan more starved and ill than the one preceding it. With the mass influx of newcomers, Afarra's streets became busier and the food sparse. The people of Afarra were urged to invite those without shelter into their homes, and hundreds of medics, farmers, fishermen and hunters were paid handsomely to heal the injured and obtain more food for the ballooning population. Several blacksmiths were recruited so those fit for battle, whether from Afarra or Tallarin, could be issued with the weapons and armour to fight. And given the lack of fight trainers in Afarra, many men took it upon themselves to train their friends in sword-handling. Soon, it wasn't just the crowded sparring areas where men fought, it was all across Afarra. And Garrin spotted children fighting with sticks on the lawns and sand too, influenced by watching their fathers and uncles.

Although joy was hard to come by in such tough times, the Afarrans were rewarded with an enjoyable new phenomenon; Sashtrams. The comical Sashtrams had been evacuated from Tallarin with the civilians. They were short, Human-like creatures with a blue tinge to their skin. Naturally inclined to serve Humans, many of the Sashtrams had been taken to the palace to aid Torvanon and his closest aides. Others though were sent out to clean the streets, cut grass, trim bushes, fix children's toys and guide the lost. But usually in the clumsiest way possible.

Outside the city, scouts travelled to and from Melzor regularly whilst small patrols of soldiers ventured into the Raspian Forest to seek out any of Jowra's own scouts. Huntsmen joined those soldiers, and they would bring back deer and rabbit to help with rations. Throughout each day, the bells above the palace would chime several times as a different party approached from across the grassy plains, returning home from whichever expedition they had just finished.

The bells also rang for the other parties from Tallarin. After Kivali and Onca led the first four-hundred evacuees through Afarra's gates, several other groups followed. Heading one of those groups was Dyma and Huadlan, a Rider and Orangutan Lavorian, while another was spearheaded by Farlog and Croij, two of the old triplets who had closely served Princess Catania before her death. But not all the people who escaped Tallarin reached Afarra safely. Two of the groups were ambushed and either killed or captured by Jowra's soldiers, while another became lost somewhere near the Piel Hills.

Garrin was grateful for all those who made it to Afarra alive, but he also craved news of Oracus. He had questioned almost every refugee, both young and old, yet none of them had seen him. Somehow, most of those people had heard the rumour that Oracus killed Catania. It seemed to be a believable story too because a lot of them wished him dead.

It was tough for Garrin to hear because he knew his friend to be kind and caring. What was harder to stomach was knowing he might be dying alone somewhere, or in need of help in one of Jowra's confines. All Garrin wanted to do was search for Oracus, but to do that would be to disobey Torvanon, and the jolly leader was relying on him for the invasion of Fervia.

To keep his mind away from Oracus, Garrin trained every day and spent a lot of time with Aquila. The attack on Fervia was to be initiated in the coming months, and Garrin had to be focused. He had already scouted Fervia, just as Alvoria had been scouted before, and he'd only seen a few Grevlor and Human patrols outside the city's stone walls. But inside the city, both Gravaz and Zarad waited patiently, a reminder that the invasion wasn't to be as simple as Garrin had hoped.

But the news that two Riders and Lavorians were guarding Fervia hadn't deterred Torvanon, it had encouraged him.

"If we kill Gravaz and Zarad and then destroy Fervia, Jowra will be on the brink of defeat," he had said happily with a thump on Garrin's back.

Garrin considered Torvanon's response to be a little over-optimistic, so he dragged himself to the training ground again to prepare some more. If he was to fight Gravaz or Zarad, or indeed Jowra himself, both he and Aquila would have to be ready for it.

"Back again, I see," a female voice called out as Garrin took to the target range with his bow. It was Kivali, and she was stood two targets along from him. With his mind elsewhere, Garrin hadn't spotted her.

"Training helps me relax and forget," he said. He flexed the string on his bow and stretched his shoulders.

A thud came as Kivali's arrow struck the centre of her target. She turned to face Garrin and offered him a shrug. "Even training doesn't help me forget. I've just learned to live with the despair."

The response wasn't what Garrin had been expecting. Usually, Kivali was full of optimism. But since arriving in Afarra, she hadn't cracked a smile once.

"You consider me weak, don't you?" she said seriously, not taking her eyes off Garrin.

Garrin frowned, for he didn't see her as weak at all. She was petite, yes, more so than usual after her arduous journey from Tallarin. But she was more than strong enough to make up for it. She was beautiful too, and a Rider with such desire that it often made Garrin feel incompetent. "No, I think you're far from weak," he said.

She raised her eyebrows. "Do you want to spar then?" she asked.

Garrin hadn't fired an arrow yet, but he felt compelled to accept. Kivali needed to vent her frustrations on someone, and it may as well be him. "With powers, or without?" he asked.

"With," she answered, and for a moment, Garrin thought he spotted a smirk.

Kivali dropped her bow and arrows and pushed past Garrin. Garrin dropped his bow too, then followed her to the fighting area adjacent to the palace. When Kivali turned, Garrin didn't allow her to set herself, and he used his power to throw a fistful of gravel at her. The attack would have covered her if she had been a lesser opponent, but she teleported quickly and kicked him in the ribs as she reappeared beside him.

Garrin dropped to his knees as Kivali teleported away. When he looked up, she was facing him from a dozen paces away, more pale and gaunt under the shadow of the palace, but resplendent in her shiny blue armour nevertheless.

"You aren't holding back, I see" he said. He rose to his feet and pulled his sword free of its sheath.

"I never do," was her response.

Kivali ran at Garrin and swung her sword at his head. He ducked under the attack and then thrust at her, but his blade was knocked aside, and she struck his leg with a whack. Garrin let out a grunt and fell.

"Come on, Garrin," Kivali said. "I need more of a challenge."

Garrin climbed from the ground for a second time. And with him, all the stones rose too as he channelled his power. As the stones floated in waiting, Garrin took a step forward and aimed a strike at Kivali's chest. She adeptly dodged his sword using her power, but the stones were too quick for her and smashed into her torso as she reappeared. The force of the attack knocked her off her feet and she landed heavily with a cry of pain.

Garrin dropped his sword and quickly crouched down to her. "Are you okay?" he asked worriedly. "Have I hurt you?"

"I'm fine," she growled, shrugging away his concerns and getting back to her feet. "Pick up your weapon. We go again."

Garrin cast Kivali an uncertain glance but reluctantly gathered his sword. She came at him again with increased vigour, and Garrin did well to evade the onslaught. He hit back with an attack of his own, but only incensed Kivali further, and she eventually caught him on the cheek with her blade. Garrin felt the skin on his face open, and he defended himself from further injury by creating a whirlwind of dust that engulfed Kivali.

"Aquila, I need your help!" he said in his mind. Within seconds, his Eagle was speeding towards him, and with a well-timed jump, he was on her back without her needing to stop. *"Up we go, girl!"* he then commanded.

Aquila spiralled into the air, leaving Kivali to fight off the whirlwind alone.

"She's dangerous with her sword," Aquila stated sternly. *"She could have really hurt you then!"*

"Don't worry, I'm sure she didn't mean to," he replied as he wiped blood from his cheek.

But Garrin soon realised he was wrong. As Aquila soared above the few fluffy clouds in the sky, a hand grasped his wrist and pulled him off his Eagle's back. It was only when Garrin was falling that he realised Kivali had teleported to meet him in the air.

His sword fell from his hand as the wind began to rush by him. "What are you doing?" he screamed as he tumbled without control. "You're going to kill us!"

"This is how Riders fight on the battlefield," Kivali yelled back. She rolled through the air towards Garrin and began to grapple with him as they fell. He received several punches to the face and more blood flowed from his cut.

"Stop this. Please!" Garrin pleaded. *"Aquila, can you catch me?"*

"I'm trying, but you're falling too fast!"

They were plummeting so quickly now that Garrin could

hear nothing but the roaring wind. He was falling with Kivali on top of him, and he surrendered to her. His body went limp, and he waited for the impact against the ground. With only seconds to go, he begged her one last time, "Kivali, save us."

He expected the end to be sudden, jarring and painful, but it wasn't. As Garrin caught sight of the ground out the corner of his eye, the world went black for a moment, and he landed softly in the meadow in the palace grounds. It took a few seconds to realise he wasn't dead, and then he breathed a deep sigh of relief. Kivali hadn't gone through with it.

"I'm okay, Aquila," he said. *"We're both okay."*

Garrin lay recumbent with Kivali slumped over him. Through windswept strands of her hair, he looked up at the sky from which he'd just fallen. "You scared me for a minute," he whispered to her.

Kivali didn't respond. But she tucked her head into his shoulder and started to cry. Garrin felt some of his anger subside, and he stroked her head with a shaky hand to comfort her.

"Do you want to talk about it?" he asked.

It took some time for Kivali to contain herself, but when she finally wiped the tears from her cheeks, she rolled off Garrin. "My life is being torn apart by Jowra," she said. "My home is now under his control, my brother was killed by his men, other friends I had have been killed by him, and now he's brainwashed Oracus."

Garrin felt a pang of sadness at hearing Oracus's name. But he didn't believe his friend had been brainwashed by the King. "Are you sure it was him who killed Catania?" he asked. "Because the Oracus I know wouldn't do that."

"I'm positive," Kivali answered. "Quent said he watched it happen. Oracus stabbed Alticon in the chest and fired an arrow through Catania's heart."

"Quent saw it?" Garrin said with surprise. "And you believe him?"

"I've known Quent far longer than I've known Oracus. And I trust that he told me the truth," Kivali stated. "He wouldn't lie about something so serious."

"And where is Quent now?" Garrin probed. "I'd like to ask him a few questions myself."

"He isn't here," Kivali said. "He was in one of the three groups that didn't make it."

"Oh, how convenient," Garrin said, rolling his eyes. "And how do you know Quent wasn't the reason that group went missing? It's probably him who works for Jowra."

Kivali's eyes suddenly welled up with more tears. "Quent is my friend and I miss him! He's a victim in this war, not a spy."

Garrin stood up and pointed his finger at Kivali. "You have it all wrong!" he said angrily. "Oracus's father was killed by Jowra's men. And his village was destroyed by them too. Do you really think he'd join him?"

"He's a Vassath Rider, Garrin. And he's the King's grandson. I hope I'm wrong, but I think he turned on us in Tallarin. The reason the city fell is because Oracus oversaw it."

Garrin dropped his voice and regained some composure. "He only joined this war because he was forced to," he said. "He became a Rider by mistake, and he knew nothing of Jowra before he came here. Oracus can get carried away sometimes, I know, but he's kind and loyal. And you would do well to find a man with more reason to end the King's life."

Kivali opened her mouth to respond, but then seemed to think better of it. Garrin took her silence as a cue to leave, and he began to wade through the meadow towards the palace. It was difficult to hold back tears of his own, for he hated that people doubted his friend without fair reason. But he reassured himself with the thought that, if Oracus wasn't dead, he would soon return and show Kivali how wrong she was. Until then, Garrin would do everything he could to bring Jowra to his knees himself.

Eight

Human Extinction

"You are too weak and slow!" Sarvon roared impatiently.

"I'm trying my best," Oracus responded, equally as frustrated.

"Then try harder."

"If I could just use a weapon or my power then I'd be more of a challenge."

"You know that is not the Ulatori way," Sarvon returned. "Fists only until you have proven yourself."

Oracus cursed under his breath. He and Sarvon were sparring in the forest under the lights of Iniril. Shurgda stood by them with a bowl of medicinal paste, ready to rub the concoction into the numerous injuries that Sarvon kept dealing to Oracus.

"You're twice my height and far stronger. What am I supposed to do?" Oracus moaned.

"You are supposed to strike me before I strike you."

Oracus spat blood onto the ground and ran at Sarvon, but the Ulatori pushed him away and watched him trip over one of Iniril's raised roots.

"I've had enough," Oracus complained from the floor. "This is pointless."

"Very well," Sarvon accepted, waving a hand dismissively. "But I expect you to improve next time." He turned to Shurgda. "Take him further into the forest and show him what he needs to know."

Shurgda nodded once and Sarvon left the clearing without looking back. Oracus stood and brushed the dirt from his clothes, then wiped the sweat from his face with a mucky hand.

"You will not beat him in a fight," Shurgda said simply.

"Then what does he expect of me?"

"He wants you to show that you are no ordinary Human," Shurgda explained. "He sees something in you because he would not waste his time otherwise. And he certainly would not risk his leadership."

"I want to prove myself to him," Oracus said. "But he's too big and strong."

"Then next time use your brain," she replied. She placed a heavy arm around Oracus's shoulder and guided him forwards. "But forget about Sarvon for now, you have other things to learn. Come with me."

Oracus accompanied Shurgda out of Iniril's light and deeper into the dark forest. The dangers of the forest concerned him, but not enough to take Sarvon off his mind. He was so desperate to impress the Ulatori leader, not just to get his approval, but so he would be allowed to leave the forest too. That day seemed a very long way off though.

"Oracus!" Shurgda hissed sharply, snapping him from his rumination. "Here."

"What have you found?" Oracus replied. He stumbled through the blackness to find her.

"It is Esa Gurar," she said, crouching down. "You must eat it."

"Esa *what?*"

"Esa Gurar. It is a plant. And it will help you see in the dark." Shurgda thrust her hand at Oracus.

"How much do I need?" Oracus asked as he took the plant from the Ulatori's fingers. It was soft and delicate.

"All of it."

Oracus grimaced as he forced petals and stem into his mouth, but the taste was surprisingly sweet, like the berries he and his father used to pick from the bushes in Thessley. It took a moment, but after swallowing, Oracus's vision improved tenfold. From seeing almost nothing in the forest, he could suddenly see everything around him in the most vibrant colours. The trees were as dense and dark as ever, their black bark like that of the ebony trees in the Raspian Forest, and their branches thick and riddled with sharp spikes. But the rest of the forest was glowing. There were fragrant flowers and healthy shrubs in the spaces between the trees, while damp mosses and large fungi grew in the deepest of shadows. Speckles of light that broke through the canopy were as dazzling as the sun itself, and a thousand pairs of eyes stared down from the highest branches above, despite there being no birdsong to hear.

"We use most of what is around us for medicines and potions," Shurgda said quietly as Oracus looked around in fascination. "Our ancestors survived on what this forest provides, and that knowledge has been passed along to us."

"Which of these flowers is Esa Gurar?" Oracus asked, looking down at the flowers around his feet.

"This." Shurgda pulled a small blue flower out the soil and held it up for Oracus to see.

Oracus took it and let it sit in his palm. From one tiny flower, the beauty and mystery of the entire forest had been revealed to him.

"What do the others do?" he asked keenly.

Shurgda picked a large golden flower with a spiky stem. "This is Artus Mor. We use the root to heal wounds, but eating the flower will make you sick." She put the Artus Mor in her satchel and then walked up to a tree with wiry grey moss on its trunk. "Oron Loib," she said wisely. "Tree's Beard. It makes for excellent tinder."

For several minutes, Shurgda plucked, named and explained the use of plants and flowers around them. Mangus Forn was a thin brown vine used for binding and tying. Ruje Marnem was a little bush, and its red leaves could be liquefied and used as a tasteless fast-acting poison. Milish was a tiny yellow weed that made its consumer feel drowsy. Larmu Ziel was a purple flower, and when rubbed on the skin, it protected against cold.

"What about this one?" Oracus asked, spotting a tall white flower with sleek long petals. "It's beautiful."

"That is Kurron," Shurgda whispered.

"And what does it do?"

Shurgda looked uneasily at Oracus, an expression he hadn't seen on her face before. "When consumed, it will disable a Rider's power and block the connection they have with their Lavorian," she said.

Oracus's eyes widened. "This is what you put in my potions?"

"It is," she answered truthfully.

Oracus wasn't sure what to say. The Ulatoris had always been honest with him about why his and Bandor's connection was cut, but suddenly seeing the flower that separated him from Bandor's mind made him angry.

"I only follow Sarvon's orders," Shurgda explained.

"What if I refused to take the potions?"

"Then I would be forced to tell Sarvon," Shurgda said.

Oracus scowled. "But why doesn't Sarvon trust me already? Why would I betray him when he spared my life?"

"He will always put the safety of his own people before another race, surely you can understand that?" she said. "But he does trust you. He would have killed you if he did not. He is just waiting for you to show that you deserve his trust."

"After how poorly I fought earlier, I doubt he'll want me alive much longer."

Shurgda gazed sympathetically at him; an honest expression that didn't suit her aggressive face, and one that helped Oracus realise he was right.

Now feeling more incompetent than ever, and angry too, he examined the pretty white flower and pulled it free of the soft ground. "We should probably take this back to the village with us then," he said miserably.

*

On a clear day in Valaroth when the snow didn't fall, the Sirin Mountains were visible in the distance, their icy peaks standing like inverted icicles above the trees of the forest. The calm, cloudless skies were a reprieve from the usual wet and windy weather, but the open skies prompted the temperature to plummet in the village.

Oracus lay on the hard bed in Shurgda's hut, reading the book Olf had lent him several days earlier. Between fidgets of mild discomfort, he flicked eagerly through the pages, intrigued by the stories within. In Thessley, he had read several fairy-tales about Humans and magical creatures, with heroes defeating mythical beasts and monsters. In this book, the stories were of similar fairy-tales, but an Ulatori was always the hero and the beasts defeated were often Humans.

Human Extinction

In a land where civilisation evolved and equality ruled, leadership was inevitably sought. Not by all, but by the Humans with their weak minds and shallow hearts. Since time first began, these creatures had craved crowns, thrones and gold, driven by their endless lust for power. Yet the other races denied them control, eager to retain peace throughout the land.

For centuries, the Humans were kept contained, until a generation in which a monster was born. A monster who cared not for his own race, nor for another, but for only himself. He was born into poverty within the realm of the Humans, but the prospect of riches soon devoured him. From existing in a place of utter hardship, he empowered himself by deceiving and stealing from those around him, and torturing and murdering those who refused to give him what he wanted.

Eventually, this Human gained the superiority to rule lesser Humans in his midst. But leadership of his own kind was not enough, and he soon sent his willing underlings to invade other realms and to defeat their leaders. From north to south, defences fell victim to his onslaught, unable to withstand his attacks, and his empire grew to a size beyond imagination. Cities were erected with unscalable walls, while an undefeatable army grew and seized control of the land. Now, the balance of the land had shifted and the equality that once ruled was lost.

With the Human on the brink of total domination, his only enemy became himself. At a time when the Human's mind was occupied wholly by the growth of his empire, he failed to see the rebellion forming within the walls of his own cities, and he forgot about those races in the forests who plotted to end his reign. But these insurgent races sought not just the death of the one tyrannous Human, they sought the extinction of the Human race as a whole.

Eventually, after years of slavery and servitude, the rebellious races sacrificed their lives for the rebirth of their land – to restore the peace and balance that had once been so selfishly taken from them. At long last, the monster and his race had been exterminated, and their thirst for power would never rise again.

Oracus gasped as the text came to an end, then he looked up at Shurgda to check she hadn't heard him. He sat up straight and swung his feet off the bed, only for a sudden chill to come over him that had nothing to do with the temperature. The tale in the book was less a story, and more a wish of the Ulatoris, Oracus suspected. Apart from Shurgda, Sarvon and Olf, the Ulatoris had made it clear what they thought of Oracus. Even though he hadn't wronged them, they still wanted him dead, and this book corroborated that. But would they really go as far as exterminating the entire Human race?

Oracus took a deep breath and lay back down. He looked up at the wooden rafters and mulled over his thoughts, which consisted mostly over whether he would ever make it out of Valaroth alive. Weeks had passed by now and still nothing had changed. The villagers still hated him, Sarvon still wanted more from him, and Bandor was still locked away in a fetid cage with all the Chagris.

The door of the hut swung open and snow came floating into the hut. The huge frame of Sarvon stooped inside and closed the door behind him.

"Are you ready to train, Rider?" he asked Oracus.

With the story still firmly on his mind, Oracus merely nodded his head.

"You look troubled," Sarvon observed.

Oracus pointed at the book. "I've read a story that ends with my race being destroyed."

Sarvon's fierce eyes met with Oracus's. "And that surprises you, does it?" he asked.

"Well, no. But it does upset me a little. We're not all like Jowra, you know."

Sarvon picked up the book and flicked through the old yellowing pages. "Whoever wrote this book would have felt the same as every other Ulatori out there." Sarvon waved a hand at the open door. "Don't let it concern you, Rider."

Oracus frowned and ran his fingers through his matted hair. Then Shurgda finished mixing herbs and sat on her stool next to the bed with two bowls in her hands.

"Oracus and I have been discussing what lives in the forest," Shurgda said to Sarvon. "He is learning well."

"Then he will know what a Yuli is?" Sarvon said quickly, placing the book down on the bed.

"It is a rare, white bird," Oracus answered, just as fast. "A Yuli will mimic the call of other creatures in the forest, even Ulatoris."

"Lifizno?" Sarvon prompted.

"Is a weed similar to the yellow Milish. But it must not be mistaken for Milish because its consumption would be deadly."

"Oron Loib?"

"Tree's Beard, it will help with making fire."

"Avolo?"

"An Avolo is like a stag. It has antlers and rich meat. It is hunted as food for the village."

"A Narborg?"

"A winged creature as black as the darkness and as silent as the falling snow. It dislikes fear but respects courage. Tarnu, your Lavorian, is a Narborg."

Sarvon smiled enthusiastically. "Very good, Rider, you *are* learning well. I am going to enter you into Alu'reath again tomorrow."

Oracus's face dropped. "Why?"

"You are getting stronger, mentally and physically," Sarvon explained. "It is another chance for you to prove yourself to the people."

"But I'm not ready yet," Oracus argued, annoyed with himself for answering all Sarvon's questions correctly. He should have known his reward would be the chance to get beaten to death by a lucky Ulatori villager.

"You are ready. And we will train together now so you can prepare."

"But–"

"He needs to take his potions before he leaves," Shurgda interrupted.

"Very well," Sarvon said as Shurgda passed Oracus his first bowl. The contents were disgusting but familiar; green, pungent and frothy. Despite his frustration, Oracus downed the potion as he did every day, and was then handed a second bowl. He lifted the bowl to his mouth, but as he was about to drink, he noticed a piece of white petal in the mixture – Kurron. Oracus looked up at Shurgda and caught her eye. She seemed timid all of a sudden, but she looked away and stole Sarvon's attention. Oracus understood what Shurgda had done, and while he had chance, he tipped the concoction down the side of the bed.

Oblivious, Sarvon turned his bald, tattooed head back towards Oracus. "Are you ready now, Rider?"

Oracus jumped up from the bed. "Yes, I am," he said, suddenly much more excited for Alu'reath.

NINE

Danzig's Defeat

With Alu'reath almost upon them, the Ulatoris in Valaroth found their voices and excited cheering could be heard throughout the snow-covered village. Oracus sat alone in Shurgda's hut listening to the din, the nervous tingling in his chest quickly becoming a sharp dagger stabbing his heart. He rocked back and forth on the bed, trying desperately to think of something other than the memory of Mechuce's giant fists smashing into his face.

Oracus might not have been so concerned had he been chosen to fight an Ulatori weaker than Mechuce, but fate had it that he would fight Danzig, an Ulatori hunter almost the size of Sarvon. Not only was Danzig big, but he was a brute too. In his last Alu'reath, he earned the right to ride a Chagri after he killed his opponent with one kick to the head.

Oracus waited for an hour until his time came to die. When a knock came at the door, Olf entered Shurgda's hut and ushered him to follow. The old Ulatori said nothing, and Oracus wondered if he was thinking that Oracus might not survive.

Oracus's stomach did a strange flip that made him sick.

He followed Olf onto the frozen path outside, wearing just his dirty rags as usual. At the sight of him, the Ulatori congregation around the square began to jeer and hiss, and a chant of *Devol Eib* could be heard over the hubbub. Oracus shivered and prayed for his life to be spared, then the crowd parted and invited him into their core.

Danzig was already waiting for Oracus, stomping around and bellowing words in the Ulatori language to his comrades. When Oracus faced him, he stopped and laughed. Then he beat his muscular chest once with his fist and pointed a threatening finger at his Human challenger.

"You will die here," he growled.

A horn blared before Oracus had prepared himself, and the Ulatori crowd was silenced. Danzig ran at Oracus and knocked him straight to the ground. Then he circled away and gave Oracus a chance to get up. The Ulatori was going to play with him.

"Are you scared, Human?" Danzig goaded. Oracus refused to reply and he bared his yellow teeth. "Very well."

The Ulatori pounced again and grabbed Oracus's leg before he had chance to flee. He was then swung around with ease and thrown into the wall of Ulatoris surrounding them. He coughed and wheezed as the air was knocked out of him, then Danzig kicked his stomach and left him gasping in pain.

"Stand up, Human!" Danzig ordered. "Face your fate."

"No, I won't play your game," Oracus said weakly.

Danzig stepped forwards and lifted him to his feet, but Oracus flopped back to the ground. The crowd rumbled with displeasure before more chants of *Devol Eib* came forth.

"Get up!" Danzig bellowed impatiently. He grabbed

Oracus again and threw him for a second time into the crowd.

On all fours, Oracus pleaded for it to be over quickly. The pain was acute now, and tears came to his eyes. But Danzig refused to end it so easily, and he aimed several kicks and punches at Oracus's body. Oracus cried out, but it only succeeded in spurring Danzig on and forcing more cheers from the crowd.

Another beating came, and then he was thrown again, this time taking the skin off his knees on the icy square. Somewhere in the distance, his senses picked up Danzig's roar of triumph. Then another sound came to him, and a ray of hope ballooned inside him.

"Oracus," came a whispering voice. *"Oracus."*

Oracus could feel a presence scratching against his mind.

"Start fighting!" The voice rose to a shout that shocked him awake.

"Bandor!" he sighed.

"If you don't get up he's going to kill you," Bandor said. *"Focus your mind."*

Oracus opened his eyes and saw Danzig towering over him. The Ulatori's palm came down and struck Oracus's face. His vision wavered.

"Ignore the pain, and focus!" Bandor urged.

Oracus felt his Lavorian delve deep inside his mind and the pain fell away.

"Do what you need to do," Bandor said.

Without the agony to distract him, Oracus could access his power again. He felt Sarvon's mind somewhere across the square and felt the mighty strength he possessed.

Danzig lifted Oracus to his feet for a final assault, and that's when Oracus made his move. Before Danzig had a chance to strike him, he used Sarvon's strength and swung a fist at the Ulatori's chin. The punch came with such force that Danzig was lifted off his feet before collapsing unconscious to the floor.

Oracus dropped to his knees as the pain in his body returned. He noticed a silence had fallen over the crowd of Ulatoris now. Through swollen eyes, he looked up and saw many expressions of shock and discontent. And there on the ground, Danzig's body lay motionless.

The minutes that followed were a blur to Oracus, and next he knew, he was back in Shurgda's hut with the healer mending his wounds and Sarvon watching over him. He kept falling in and out of consciousness, until eventually several hours had passed. But throughout it all, not once did Sarvon leave his side.

*

"What about my bow?" Oracus asked as he sheathed his sword and tucked his dagger into his belt.

"That is here," Sarvon answered, lifting the bow for Oracus to see.

"I can use it all now?" he asked, wanting confirmation.

"As promised," Sarvon replied.

"Great. I won't wear my armour here though. I don't want any Ulatoris feeling uncomfortable," Oracus said wisely. "But can I pick some Larmu Ziel from the forest to keep me warm?"

"Of course."

Oracus let his fingers touch the emerald of his sword and smiled. Finally he had proven himself to Sarvon and had his belongings returned to him. He was sat at the square table in Sarvon's stone home with the warmth of the embers in the fireplace dancing over him. Sarvon was stood behind the table, leaning against the back of his chair, a black fur robe draped over his shoulders.

"Can Bandor be let out his cage now?" Oracus asked him.

The Ulatori pondered the question but shook his head, "No, not yet."

Oracus was disappointed but knew it was for the best of the village. "But we can train together in the forest, right?"

"You can if I am there to observe."

"Can we go now?"

"You still have a schedule to follow, Rider. You are to speak with Olf today."

"Fine," Oracus conceded. "But what about tomorrow?"

Sarvon grunted impatiently, then rounded the table and began adding wood to the fire. He didn't answer Oracus's question, but eventually asked his own. "How did you defeat Danzig yesterday?"

The guilt came to Oracus immediately and he looked away from the Ulatori. "It must have been luck."

"Do not consider me a fool, Rider," Sarvon stated, fixing Oracus with a serious stare. "Only once have I seen Danzig beaten, and that is when I beat him myself. There was quite a resemblance between my victory and yours."

"That's because I copied your strength," Oracus admitted. "My power is to copy that of others."

"Have you not been taking Shurgda's potions?" Sarvon enquired.

"I didn't drink one when I saw it had Kurron in it."

"You went behind my back," Sarvon claimed. "For that, I should punish you. Most of the villagers here would want you killed if they found out what you did."

"Are you going to punish me?" Oracus asked worriedly.

"Do you think you would have defeated Danzig without your power?" Sarvon questioned.

"No, I would have been killed," Oracus said honestly.

"Then I am glad you chose not to drink your potion because all your training would have been for nothing." Sarvon stepped away from the fire and gently ruffled Oracus's hair. "I have been teaching you to think like a Rider, and finally you have done. I cannot punish you for that."

"Thank you," Oracus sighed.

"Remember that politeness is weakness," Sarvon reminded.

"I'm sorry," Oracus added.

Sarvon scowled and Oracus let out a guilty laugh.

"I am looking forward to training with a *Rider* now," Sarvon said. "It has been a while since I have been tested."

TEN

Improving A Power

Oracus followed Sarvon to the area where Bandor was confined to his cage alongside dozens of Chagris. When they arrived, the grunts and snarls of the hog-like creatures began, and they thrashed around inside their enclosures.

"Don't get too close to them," Sarvon warned. "They haven't been fed since yesterday."

Oracus paid heed and kept away from the black-eyed Chagris until he was beside Bandor's cage.

"Good morning," he said aloud, smiling happily at the sight of the Lion.

"Good morning," came the enthusiastic reply.

Sarvon opened the lock on the cage and Bandor strolled out and stretched. He had grown considerably since their arrival in Valaroth, to almost the height of the Ulatori leader beside them, and his mane was fuller and more prominent than before. In the white world around them, his armour coat shone magnificently, and his amber eyes dazzled like fire.

"Are you ready to train, Lavorian?" Sarvon asked.

"Anything to get out this cage," Bandor replied.

"Then come with us. Tarnu is waiting in the forest."

"What will she teach me?" Bandor quizzed.

"To open your mind," Sarvon explained as he marched them away from the Chagris. "Like your Rider, it has been narrowed."

"What do you mean?"

"A Rider and Lavorian should be one mind combined, but you two remain apart. You are connected by only a fraction of your potential."

"And what is our potential?" Oracus asked curiously.

"Tarnu and I are linked even now," Sarvon explained. "I use her heightened senses so I can see, hear, smell and feel far more than you can. That is why I knew of the Narborg following us in the forest on your first day of training. It is also how I was aware of you trespassing in the forest those many weeks ago."

"So how do we connect like that?" Oracus probed.

"That is what you will be taught in the forest," Sarvon expressed.

They passed through the first trees of the forest and the daylight was immediately quenched. As normal, a spooky silence fell over Oracus, with only their footsteps to be heard.

"Thank you for your help in Alu'reath," Oracus said secretly to Bandor.

"That's why I'm here," Bandor replied modestly. *"How did you regain our connection?"*

"I didn't drink one of the potions Shurgda gave to me."

"Very smart," Bandor praised.

"It was Shurgda actually," Oracus admitted. *"She told me of Kurron's power then didn't grind it down properly in one of my potions. She did it on purpose so I wouldn't drink it."*

"She helped you get your power back?"

"She must have known my fate in Alu'reath. If my power hadn't come back then Danzig would surely have killed me."

They trudged through the undergrowth behind Sarvon, following the Ulatori's enormous silhouette. They were heading towards Iniril; even in the intense darkness Oracus knew the route.

"And was it you who took away my pain?" Oracus continued.

"Yes, but it wasn't pleasant," Bandor replied.

"You could feel it?"

"I was just doing what Aquila taught me back in Afarra. I borrowed your pain so you could concentrate on what you needed to do."

"Thank you," Oracus said gratefully. He felt a surge of pride come from within his Lavorian's mind. *"Shurgda isn't the only one who saved my life, you've done it too. And more than once. I will repay you one day."*

The silver glow of Iniril broke through the trees after several minutes, and speckles of pink blossom fell on them as they entered the clearing. Bandor's eyes rose to the canopy and his mouth dropped open.

"Quite something, isn't it?" Oracus said, still in awe himself despite having visited the tree several times already.

"I wasn't expecting to see something so beautiful here," Bandor replied.

Sarvon had reached Iniril's trunk by the time Oracus spotted Tarnu in the clearing with them. The Narborg Lavorian was an impressive beast, with six muscular legs and a giant head that somewhat resembled that of a wolf. Tarnu was taller than Sarvon, and she was so long from nose to tail that Bandor appeared small in comparison. Her metal armour was the same as Bandor's, but her claws were twice as long.

"May we start training, Rider?" Sarvon shouted across the clearing.

Oracus and Bandor approached Iniril themselves, being careful not to trip on any of the raised roots. Tarnu watched them with interest, her fierce green eyes shining like the emerald in Oracus's sword.

"Rider, you will come with me, as usual," Sarvon explained. "Lavorian, you will train with Tarnu."

Oracus was drawn to the memory of Tarnu holding a limp Bandor between her teeth when they had first been captured. There on Valaroth's square, Oracus had thought his Lavorian dead.

"I'll be fine," Bandor assured, reading Oracus's concern.

Sarvon and Oracus left Bandor and Tarnu and headed for the dark treeline. "You said you can copy the powers of other Riders. Is that right?" Sarvon asked.

Oracus nodded faintly, well aware of how others had reacted to that news in the past.

"Vassath Riders are very rare," Sarvon said. "And very dangerous too."

"I've heard that before," Oracus said.

"It is a skill you share with Jowra," Sarvon added. "So I must stress that you keep it to yourself. None of my villagers can know."

Oracus hadn't intended to share with anyone his likenesses with the King, so it was easy for him to agree.

"Now you are able to mimic my power," Sarvon said, pushing beyond talk of Jowra. "You should be competitive in a fight with me."

"I don't think you should worry about that," Oracus said.

But the words had barely left his mouth when Sarvon tackled him to the floor.

The wind was knocked out of Oracus as he landed across a jagged root, but he scrambled away before Sarvon could grab him again. He groaned as he pushed himself to his feet, then ducked under Sarvon's advance and side-stepped a fierce kick. Several punches came next and Oracus dodged them deftly, but eventually a fist found its mark and Oracus dropped to his knees.

"Are you in pain already?" the Ulatori snapped unhappily.

The terrible ache in his chest stopped Oracus from answering.

"Maybe it was luck that helped you defeat Danzig," Sarvon said. "Because even an ordinary Ulatori would beat you like this."

Oracus was certain it *was* luck that had helped him defeat Danzig. The Ulatoris were all twice his size; even without powers they were formidable. He wouldn't choose to fight any of them, not even Shurgda.

"You aren't giving me a chance," he wheezed through broken breaths.

"Do you think your enemies will give you a chance in battle?" Sarvon enquired with a shake of his head. "Maybe you will improve now you know how much it hurts."

But when Sarvon came again, Oracus barely had the time to rise from his knees. Within a moment, his torso was being clenched in Sarvon's fist. The Ulatori held him there for a moment, his yellow teeth bared, then he threw Oracus into the air as if he were no heavier than a stick.

Oracus landed with a sickening crunch.

*

Tarnu was a huge Lavorian. Even after months of growing inside his cage, Bandor was still dwarfed by her. Maybe he would no longer fit comfortably between her jaws like he had in Valaroth's square, but he was sure she would overpower him in a fight.

"How long have you been with your Rider?" Tarnu asked in a throaty rasp.

"More than a year now," Bandor answered.

"Explain to me the strength of your bond."

Bandor considered the question for a moment. "We can talk with our minds," he said.

"That is all?"

"And we can see through each other's eyes," Bandor added.

Tarnu flicked her tail impatiently. "You are weaker than I had expected."

"Weaker?" Bandor asked, somewhat aggrieved.

"Yes, far weaker. As Sarvon explained before, a Rider and Lavorian should be as one. You provide almost no help to your Rider. You should always be in control of his mind, and always know what he is feeling. In return, he should always have access to your senses and voice."

"That seems like a lot."

"It will not be easy at first. You will have to keep the connection with your Rider at the forefront of your mind. But eventually it will become less difficult, and then the link will be there without you even realising."

"How do I make the link now?" Bandor asked.

Tarnu's tail swayed again. "When you are speaking to your Rider, it means you have entered his mind. Once you have made this link, you can delve further."

Bandor closed his eyes and focused on Oracus's mind. He rummaged for a few seconds but only felt the same dull throb he always seemed to feel when he was in Oracus's head. He switched his attention back to Tarnu. "All I feel is pain."

"That is because your Rider is feeling pain. He is no match for Sarvon."

Bandor shook himself and then connected to Oracus once more. The pain arrived again but this time Bandor somehow swept the feeling to one side. With his mind free, he was able to push his heightened senses into Oracus's mind. But when he thought he was beginning to aid Oracus, something struck him hard across the head. He growled and opened his eyes, only to find Tarnu ready to lash him for a second time with her tail.

"Never lose focus on what is in front of you, Lavorian. If I were your enemy, you would now be dead."

*

"Tell me how you make your power work," Sarvon prompted Oracus.

"I have to link my mind to yours before I can summon the power," Oracus answered. "I can only use the power properly if I think of nothing else."

"So you cannot just use it like any other Rider can?"

Oracus shook his head, "I don't think so."

"I see," Sarvon said thoughtfully.

"And it helps if I've seen the other Rider's power before I copy it."

"But you didn't know of my power before you struck

Danzig in Alu'reath."

"I seem to be fortunate in moments of despair," Oracus explained.

"Or maybe your body is finding a way for you to show your true strength," Sarvon suggested.

"How do you mean?"

"Rider, what emotions are you feeling right now?"

"I'm not sure," Oracus said.

"Are you feeling lonely? You *are* in a village that is far away from the people you know and love."

"I guess so," Oracus replied.

"Are you feeling angry or upset because you are being kept in Valaroth when you don't want to be here?"

"I–" Oracus began, but Sarvon continued.

"Are you mourning the loss of your parents? Mourning the loss of your friends? Are you confused about what Pharia has taught you since you left your little village in the forest? Are you frightened of me? Frightened of my comrades? Frightened of death?"

Oracus stared at Sarvon, unsure of how he should reply.

"Do you feel any of these emotions, Rider?" Sarvon forced.

"I feel them all," Oracus admitted. "But I don't understand why it's relevant."

"Because a Rider's power is strongest when he has no emotions to cloud his mind," Sarvon explained. "In moments of despair, like you felt in Alu'reath, all your emotions, except despair, are lost. And in those moments, your power is stronger than it ever has been before."

What Sarvon said made sense, Oracus thought. Since bonding with Bandor, he had known nothing but pain. His father's death had come first, then the battle at Tallarin and the loss of his mother, and now he was being held in Valaroth where he feared for his life. Maybe that was why he had struggled to discover his power at the beginning, and why training and developing it had been so slow. Come to think of it, those times he'd used his power by mistake was when his mind had been narrowed. First, it was the calmness of the council room in Afarra, then it was when he faced Gravaz and feared for his life.

Oracus looked at Sarvon, who had allowed himself a rare grin. "So how am I to stop my emotions?" he asked.

"It is much easier to explain than it is to do," Sarvon said. "You can either learn to forget your feelings, or you can rely on your Lavorian."

"How can Bandor help?" Oracus asked.

"He can be taught to force your emotions upon himself and leave you with a free mind."

"Like he can with my pain?"

"Exactly," Sarvon said. "And it will make your power the strongest it can be."

"When should we practise that?"

"It is for your Lavorian to learn alone, Rider. In fact, I believe that is what Tarnu is teaching him now."

ELEVEN

Saving A Life

Training under the glow of Iniril continued for several weeks. Oracus and Bandor were definitely improving, yet overpowering Sarvon or Tarnu still seemed a very long way off. With Sarvon's guidance, Oracus had begun to master his power. For the most part, he could use Sarvon's strength without too much thought, which left the rest of his brain free to think about how to dodge the Ulatori's powerful kicks and punches.

Meanwhile, Bandor had thrived under Tarnu's strict tuition. Oracus constantly felt the Lion in his mind, making loud his voice and projecting both his thoughts and senses. This was most useful when Oracus was fighting Sarvon, but Bandor expressed his mind even when Oracus was relaxing in Shurgda's hut. *A Rider and their Lavorian should always be connected,* Sarvon and Tarnu kept repeating. So Oracus would often receive a bright surge of light while he was falling asleep, or hear the distant snorts of Chagris ripping apart an Avolo in the depths of the forest.

Bandor had also learnt to consume Oracus's emotions. This enabled his power to be as efficient as possible. When this happened, Oracus felt nothing: there was no sorrow, no hurt, no hate, no love. It was a relief for sure, but the emptiness inside was a strange feeling.

Not everything was about Oracus's skill in combat though. Yes, the sparring seemed to be for Oracus's physical improvement – a way for Sarvon to show Oracus how he should use his body to bully and his mind to outthink his enemies. But Oracus was sure the Ulatori was developing him as a person just as much. Their breaks from sparring would always involve tests of knowledge, in which Oracus would have to name plants and animals of the forest. He was also shown how to mimic animal calls, tie different knots, forecast the weather (which was almost always snow), stalk and kill the stag-like Avolo in the forest, and then cook it for the Ulatoris in the village. It was these skills that had triggered the biggest change in Oracus, for he now felt comfortable and safe in a place where he had once been lonely and vulnerable. Several long months had passed in Valaroth, and aside from the villagers still not accepting him, it was beginning to feel much like home.

On a particularly snowy and windy day, Oracus left Shurgda's hut to visit Bandor in his cage. Since his victory over Danzig in Alu'reath, the Ulatoris no longer jeered at Oracus, but they still offered him disapproving looks as he walked through the village. When he had almost reached the cages where Bandor and the Chagris were held, a faint noise being carried on the strong winds caught his heightened senses.

"Bandor, did you hear that?" he asked his Lavorian.

"Hear what?" was the reply.

"I don't know. It was too quiet for me to tell."

"I didn't hear anything, Oracus. I think all this training is messing with your ears."

"But I'm sure–" He cupped a hand over his ear. *"Wait, I heard it again!"*

The second sound had been as soft as the first. But it was enough to make Oracus step off the path towards the forest. The black trees loomed over him, but he stood unmoving for a full minute without catching the noise again.

"You must be imagining it," Bandor said. *"I can't hear anything but the wind."*

"I think you're right," Oracus surrendered. But as he turned back to find the path, the sound came again, and this time it was louder and sounded like a plea for help.

"Well that definitely wasn't your imagination," Bandor admitted. But Oracus was already bounding into the trees. *"Be careful in there,"* the Lion added.

"Just stay in my mind, Bandor."

"I always am."

The denseness of the forest Oracus knew only too well. He pushed through the bushes and undergrowth as fast as he could, with Bandor's sight helping him to see any obstacles he should duck under or hurdle. He stopped for a moment to wait for the call again, and this time he heard a shout of fear. Oracus pressed on, but a nervousness fluttered in his stomach.

The sound of running water was next to find Oracus's ears, and he burst into a clearing to find a narrow waterfall that dropped into a deep, dark gorge. Snow was falling in heavy flakes through the opening in the canopy above, and the thicket around the gorge was hidden under a thick blanket of white.

Oracus's heart dropped at the sight that met him. The rocks of the waterfall were slippery wet, and several huge icicles hung into the depths of the gorge. But there, clinging to the rocks by his fingertips, an Ulatori who had fallen over the edge.

The wind whistled through the trees as Oracus considered his next move. Shouts of despair came from the Ulatori too, and Oracus urged him to hold on.

Focusing on Sarvon's power, Oracus gathered the strength he needed to pull a lonely sapling from the ground. When it came free, he moved carefully to edge of the gorge and dangled the tree over the edge.

"Grab on to this!" Oracus yelled. "I'll pull you up."

The Ulatori refused the help. "I-would-rather-die-than-trust-Human," he said stubbornly.

"I'll save you. I promise!"

The Ulatori turned his face away and Oracus cursed. He cast the sapling aside and walked further along the gorge.

"I hope you aren't planning a suicidal rescue mission," Bandor's voice echoed in his head.

"It's not suicidal," Oracus said.

"It looks quite suicidal to me."

Oracus glanced fearfully over the edge of the gorge and could barely see the bottom, even with Bandor's vision aiding him. He could just about see where the falling water crashed onto the jagged rocks.

"I need you to take away my emotions, Bandor," Oracus said, remembering his training with Sarvon. *"I'm going to need the full strength of my power."*

Oracus momentarily felt Bandor's concern, but then all the fear subsided as the Lavorian obliged.

After taking a moment to compose himself, Oracus edged his way to the rocks at the very top of the waterfall. Then he concentrated on Sarvon's power again and began the descent down the waterfall's face.

With the strength of one-hundred men, the climbing wasn't so hard, but the icy water took Oracus's breath away and the wet rocks moved and crumbled under his weight.

"Take away my pain too, Bandor," he urged. *"This water is freezing."*

He slowly clambered down towards the Ulatori, whose hands and feet slipping perilously with every movement.

"Now will you let me help you?" he shouted through mouthfuls of water when the Ulatori was in reach.

"Leave-me-alone," the Ulatori bellowed back. But in the same second, he lost his grip and Oracus caught his arm to stop him falling.

"Shall I leave you alone now?" Oracus said.

The Ulatori looked down at the rocks below, then glanced back up at Oracus, his yellow eyes wide.

"Just hold still," Oracus asserted.

He looked over his shoulder to check the distance to the edge of the gorge, secured his footing on the wet rock beneath his feet, and then jumped with all Sarvon's might. The rock cracked as he leapt, but held firm, and the gorge threatened to consume them as they sailed over it. But then Oracus and the Ulatori landed on solid, snowy ground.

Intense relief and joy came back to Oracus as Bandor withdrew from his mind, and then he started shivering as the cold bit at his wet skin.

"See, it wasn't suicidal," he said with a laugh to Bandor. He pulled the Ulatori from the floor and slung him over his shoulder, then clambered back through the forest towards the village.

*

The impact of Oracus's life saving rescue wasn't immediate, but during the following day his reward arrived. Early in the morning he was sat in Shurgda's hut, having just eaten, and a knock came at the door. The door opened and a gust of powdery snow circled the room until the door slammed shut. Stepping inside was the Ulatori from the waterfall. Following the incident, Oracus had learned that the Ulatori's name was Yox, and he was a hunter.

The sudden appearance of Yox left Oracus in a state of shock. Since he had arrived in Valaroth all those months ago, Yox was the only Ulatori, other than Sarvon, Shurgda and Olf, to have voluntarily entered Shurgda's hut with Oracus inside.

Yox was of a stocky build. He was shorter than the average Ulatori, but somehow wider at the shoulders. Despite the freezing weather, his chest was bare, and his muscles looked like they were about to burst out his skin. His bearded face was fierce, but not filled with the hatred Oracus had become so accustomed to. Strapped to his back was a wooden bow and a quiver full of arrows, and in his hands was a brown, leather contraption. After he shook the snow from his shoulders, he thrust the contraption at Oracus and grunted.

"It-is-saddle," Yox stammered in broken speech as Oracus accepted the device and studied it. "I-do-not-like-to-owe."

Oracus's confusion turned to gratitude. He would have thanked the Ulatori, but to do so would show weakness, so he bowed his head instead.

"Come," Yox said. With his hand, he beckoned Oracus to follow him and exited Shurgda's hut. Oracus strode curiously after him, still clutching the heavy saddle in his arms.

The Ulatori led Oracus to Bandor's cage (*"Good morning,"*) and opened the lock. Without speaking, Yox seized the saddle from Oracus and began to attach it to Bandor's torso. He fitted the straps around each of his legs and under his belly, set the seat in the middle of his back, then adjusted the knots until it fit Bandor perfectly.

"It looks great," Oracus said enthusiastically.

Yox nodded his head, satisfied, then marched back into the village without a word.

"I think you're gaining their trust," Bandor observed.

"I think you're right," Oracus answered, pleased with himself. *"And now I can ride you without my legs getting sore."*

He admired Yox's handiwork for a moment and then patted Bandor on the nose. Knowing at least one more Ulatori didn't hate him was a very good feeling indeed.

TWELVE

Iniril's Rage

The next time Oracus was training beneath the lights of Iniril, Sarvon was in the best mood Oracus had seen. Perhaps it was because another blizzard was arriving, or maybe it was because Oracus had finally gained some respect amongst his people – exactly what the Ulatori had been hoping would happen for several months.

"Now that you have a saddle, it would be a shame not to teach you to ride," Sarvon said, motioning at Bandor. He may have been cheery, but he was still as pushy as ever. "Climb on."

Bandor dropped helpfully onto his belly, and Oracus swung a leg over his back. He perched himself on Yox's leather saddle and pressed his feet into the stirrups. Bandor rose to his feet.

"Firstly," Sarvon expressed, "be careful of low hanging branches."

Oracus nodded.

"Secondly, always keep your minds connected when you ride. It is crucial that you both understand where you are going and why. This way you will not make a wrong turn."

Oracus smiled to himself, pleased that this part of

training allowed him to be so close to Bandor.

"Well, what are you waiting for?" Sarvon bellowed. He slapped Bandor's rump with a strong hand. "Go!"

Bandor didn't need to be told twice. He bounded excitedly over the roots of Iniril and into the trees. The cold air was soon rushing through Oracus's hair and the snow that crept through the canopy was striking his bare hands and face. Bandor forced his mind into Oracus's and shared his intended route, just as Sarvon had suggested. And with that, Oracus could lean effectively into every sharp turn and duck safely under any obstacles. The riding was jolting at first, but after a minute or so, Oracus pushed himself out the saddle with his legs so he didn't bounce so uncomfortably with each of Bandor's strides. The ecstasy he felt within his and Bandor's combined minds was exhilarating, enhanced all the more by their recent separation.

From above, a piercing screech came to their ears and Oracus looked up. The silver underbelly of Tarnu was flickering above the gaps in the forest's canopy, her six dangling claws almost scraping the tops of the trees. Sarvon was riding her, and he was glancing down at the path Oracus and Bandor were carving through the trees.

Bandor pressed on, gathering more speed until they returned to where they had begun. The glow of Iniril burst through the trees and they skidded to a halt at its trunk. But then another shriek came and Tarnu rocketed towards them from above. She collided heavily with Bandor's side and sent Oracus tumbling helplessly across the clearing.

When he picked himself up, he groaned unhappily. The skin on his knees and elbows had been shredded on the roots around him and he'd banged his leg on something hard.

"Bandor, are you okay?" he quizzed with his mind.

There was no reply.

"Bandor?" He looked up from his wounds and saw that his Lavorian and Tarnu had crashed into the dense trees and out of sight.

A roar escaped the forest and the hairs on Oracus's neck stood up. He started running to where Bandor had vanished, but a giant hand grabbed his wrist and threw him through the air. He hit the trunk of Iniril hard, and the wind was knocked out of his lungs.

"What are you doing?" Oracus wheezed as Sarvon bared down on him. But when the Ulatori grabbed his legs and threw him across the clearing again without a word, Oracus realised it was another test. Oracus rose to his feet and readied himself for what was to come. He faced the tattooed Ulatori and waited for him to begin his next attack.

The snarl that Sarvon offered was terrifying in itself, but Oracus was able to dodge the first punches the Ulatori threw. He stumbled backwards, ducked under another strike, but then succumbed to a kick in the chest that left him recumbent.

Oracus found his feet once more and focused on Sarvon's power, but without Bandor's help, the fear and pain flowed wildly through his body and made him weak. Where was his Lavorian, and why wasn't he responding?

Sarvon closed in again and Oracus made the decision to run, for he would never beat Sarvon in one-on-one combat anyway, not even with full use of his power. He needed to be smart and cunning to defeat his stronger opponent, so his best chance was to try something unusual.

He looked around the clearing purposefully as he fled, and then looked up at Iniril above. The tree's lowest branches were high, but within reach if he used Sarvon's power to jump. The Ulatori's heavy stomps were soon catching up with him, so Oracus triggered the power and leaped. Thankfully, he was just able to cling to one of the thinner branches and pull himself up.

Several metres below, Sarvon stared up at him. "Why are you running away?" the Ulatori shouted.

Now it was Oracus's turn to keep his silence. He immediately started climbing further up the tree, just like he had so many times in the Raspian Forest as a child, and willed Sarvon to follow.

Higher and higher he ascended, all the time wondering if Sarvon was climbing beneath him, until he broke through the canopy of the smaller trees and found himself engulfed by light. Rising from the darkness was heavenly, and from such a height, he could see so much more than he'd expected to. The forest seemed so calm from above, despite the blizzard approaching from the south. The frosted black leaves of one tree would entwine with the leaves of several of its neighbours for miles into the distance, and there was so little wind, not a branch was stirring. To the south-east, Oracus could see the shimmering ocean he and Bandor had floated across when they first came to the Black Forest. And to the north-west, the impressive Sirin Mountains stood tall and handsome with their icy caps.

The sound of snapping branches below made Oracus start. He tore his eyes from the magnificent view and looked up at Iniril's highest branches. He still had a long way to go, so he persevered tenaciously, and hoped that Sarvon wouldn't catch him before he got there.

The higher Oracus climbed, the weaker the branches became, and the more careful he had to be with his feet. The wind that had been absent below suddenly revealed itself in gusts that swayed the entire tree, and Oracus questioned more and more if his plan was a wise one.

As he reached the topmost branches, which were barely thick enough to hold his weight, he finally looked down. His legs buckled when he saw Iniril oscillating beneath him, and he shivered as the first of the blizzard's snowflakes touched his face. Oracus realised he'd never been so high in all his life, and it was a terrifying feeling. What was more, he could now see Sarvon climbing to meet him, and that only made him more scared. There was nowhere to hide up here.

"I could really use your help now, Lavorian," Oracus said through his mind, urging Bandor to respond.

There was still no response, but Oracus instantly felt his fear subside. Bandor was no doubt still fighting Tarnu, but able to spare a bit of his mind to assist Oracus.

With his fear now eradicated by Bandor, Oracus waited for Sarvon to meet him and then walked bravely away from Iniril's trunk along a thin branch. With nothing to hold on to, he focused on keeping his balance, and when Sarvon stepped onto the same branch, he almost fell as it lurched.

"There is nowhere else to run now, Rider," the Ulatori announced triumphantly.

Oracus pointed downwards with his finger. "But there is." He cupped his hands over his mouth and released a screech that mimicked a Narborg. Then he jumped on the branch and forced it to snap beneath his and Sarvon's feet.

Sarvon roared as they dropped perilously towards the

other trees beneath them, but Oracus barely flinched. The wind rushed through his hair, but he was never fearful of dying.

As the black approached, Oracus manoeuvred himself towards Sarvon and wrapped his arms as far around the Ulatori's thick waist as he could. Then, as they crashed through the first leaves of the forest canopy, a winged creature with green eyes soared after them and caught them both firmly in its claws. In an instant, Bandor left Oracus's mind and relief flooded his body.

The Narborg swooped in a circular descent around Iniril's glowing trunk until they safely reached the forest floor. When the Narborg let them go, Oracus rolled onto Sarvon and held him face down in the dirt.

"Impressive," came a mutter from the Ulatori's mouth.

Oracus waited a few seconds and then removed his hands from the Ulatori. They both stood up shakily.

"Very impressive," Sarvon repeated. He laughed loudly and the tattoos on his grey face contorted like Oracus hadn't seen before.

Oracus laughed too and gratefully stroked the Narborg's head. The spines covering the surface of its jet-black body quivered with pleasure and it pressed its snout into Oracus's hand.

"What made you think of using a Narborg?" Sarvon enquired, still breathing heavily.

"I know I can't defeat you one-on-one. I'm not strong enough," Oracus explained. "And other than Bandor, this Narborg is all I can rely on in the forest. You told me she would never forget me, and I trusted that you were right."

"You've shown true character today, Oracus."

Oracus looked at Sarvon in surprise. The Ulatori had

never called him by name.

"Perhaps you would be willing to pray to Iniril?" Sarvon proposed.

"Oh, I don't think so," Oracus stated. He was still unsure about praying to a tree that meant so much to the Ulatoris, and so little to him.

"I think you have proved you are as much an Ulatori as a Human can be," Sarvon claimed. "It would be an honour if you did."

Sarvon's words made Oracus feel somewhat obliged. He studied Iniril and then moved closer to the base where the roots were thickest. He reached out a hand, clenched a damp root in his fist, and closed his eyes. A steady stream of whispers floated into his head, fluttering calmly between his ears, until a ferocious lurch of the ground threw Oracus from his feet and he lost contact with the root. The enormous tree creaked and moved, and everything in the clearing trembled violently. The once silver glow of Iniril had turned to an enraged blood red, and a chilling voice resonated from the trunk.

"Jowra… Jowra… JOWRA…"

The tree seemed to be alive, and it smashed its branches into the ground furiously, forcing Oracus to shield himself with his arms and back away. He watched the wild Narborg gallop away from the clearing, and then spotted Sarvon trying to keep his balance on the undulating floor. Iniril's long, flexible roots ripped themselves from the ground and slithered through the air as if searching for something.

"Jowra's blood is here…" the voice echoed louder. "…Kill the Human… Jowra's blood! … KILL THE HUMAN… JOWRA'S BLOOD! …" The tree was now bent almost double. It had uprooted dozens of trees around it and was throwing them across the clearing with its branches and roots.

"You need to get out of here, Rider!" Oracus heard Sarvon shout. "Leave the forest now. Travel north and don't look back! I trust you to fulfil our agreement."

A large branch swung at Oracus and knocked him to the ground. But with Sarvon's offer of freedom ringing clearly in his ears, he pulled himself resolutely back to his feet. When he looked for the Ulatori leader, he was gone, lost somewhere beyond Iniril's reach. All Oracus could see now were the tree's flailing appendages, and Bandor bounding elegantly between them. The Lion was heading for Oracus, determined to reach his Rider and escort him from danger.

Another of Iniril's branches swiped Oracus's feet from under him, but before a fatal blow could be landed, Bandor snatched Oracus from the ground with his teeth and raced out the clearing.

For several minutes, Bandor ran with Oracus bouncing limply in his jaws. It was only when they could no longer hear Iniril uprooting neighbouring trees that they stopped. And even then, they didn't dare linger too long in the darkness.

Thirteen

Ice And Snow

Jowra's eyes widened in surprise. A sharp, stabbing sensation built inside him that he hadn't felt for almost six decades. An anger emerged from within the tree of the Black Forest and he could feel it so acutely. The fury it unleashed was greater even than the time he had stolen part of its power those many years ago.

But what had caused it to react so violently? Jowra steadied himself and called upon every piece of his extraordinary mind.

Crimson light shone upon the forest floor and nearby trees. Swelling roots moved in the earth and caused the ground to tremor. Loose leaves fell through the dusty air, while insects and birds darted this way and that to avoid the branches that flashed dangerously in all directions. Jowra's vision flickered between the keep in his palace and Iniril in the Black Forest. He focused harder, squinting as he scanned his surroundings, hoping to catch a glimpse of what was causing Iniril's distress.

And there he was – the Vassath Rider. The boy who Jowra had wished was dead. The boy who had apparently met his end in Tallarin – or so Gravaz had claimed. He was standing motionless in a dark clearing, his eyes as red as Jowra's as they reflected Iniril's rage. But the boy seemed helpless, as rooted to the forest floor as Iniril itself. It seemed for all the world he would succumb to one of the branches, and Jowra silently pleaded for it, but every swipe of the huge tree's appendages missed its mark.

Then eventually, one branch caught his legs and he fell. But the Lavorian was quick to assist and scooped up his Rider in his jaws. In seconds, the boy and his Lion were out of sight, and all that remained in the clearing was churned earth and Iniril's scarlet glow.

Jowra's vision faded as his frustration grew, and he let out a roar that made even his Dragons quiver in fear.

*

The ground continued to rumble and quake, even when Oracus and Bandor were several miles north. It had been hours since their flight from Valaroth, but Iniril was still thrashing around in anger.

It was a relief for Oracus to finally be heading home, but the regret he felt for having to leave the Ulatoris under such circumstances hampered his elation. For several months it had been his deepest wish to escape the forest, but having recently gained the trust of Yox, he felt the timing of his forced flight couldn't have been worse. Just a few more weeks and he was sure many of the other Ulatoris would have learned to trust him too.

"Who would have thought when we arrived here that you'd be sad to leave," Bandor said, reading Oracus's mind.

Oracus sat in his Lavorian's saddle, rubbing the root of Artus Mor into the cuts that Iniril had dealt him. He watched steam rise from the wounds as they sealed. *"It would have been nice to say goodbye to Shurgda and Olf after all they did for me,"* he replied.

But it wasn't just the upset of having to leave Valaroth that concerned Oracus. Worryingly, he'd had another vision of Jowra, the first he'd suffered since leaving Tallarin. And since the vision, he'd experienced spurts of anger he wouldn't usually feel, as if Jowra's emotions were somehow living within him. Oracus hadn't discussed these feelings with Bandor, but neither did he have to. His Lion could read him like a book these days, and he sensed the anger every time it arose.

They pushed on as fast as they could, but the forest was so overgrown in places that they would struggle to cover a mile in an hour. The further away they travelled from Valaroth, the denser the trees became, and the spikier their branches. Whenever Oracus spotted Artus Mor growing in the undergrowth, he would jump from Bandor's back to pick it. It seemed every few minutes he would have a fresh cut to heal. He also pocketed as much Larmu Ziel and Esa Gurar as he could. The purple flower helped protect his skin from the cold, while the small blue flower kept him alert in the darkness.

For the entire day, they pressed on, until they finally reached the northernmost point of the forest where the trees thinned. It surprised Oracus that they hadn't encountered a pack of Chagris, for Sarvon had always warned him of how keen the beasts were for Human flesh. And it surprised him further that not one flake of snow had fallen all day, despite it seeming colder.

Oracus squinted as they reached the vast expanse of whiteness that followed the forest. Ice and snow covered the land for as far into the distance as Oracus could see, with not even a shrub or hill to disrupt the landscape to the north. To the west, the Sirin Mountains reached high into the sky, their snowy peaks disappearing into the lowest of the wintry clouds.

"Come on, Bandor," Oracus urged. He patted his Lion's head encouragingly. *"We can get across this in no time."*

Bandor increased his speed. *"It feels good to finally be out the darkness,"* he said with satisfaction.

Oracus inhaled a deep breath. *"It definitely feels fresher out here,"* he said.

Bandor's walk became a gallop and his metal paws threw up clouds of powdery snow behind them. Upon his back, Oracus grimaced as the cold open air began to bite the skin on his face.

"I can't wait to see Garrin," Oracus said, pushing his blonde hair out his face with numb fingers. *"It's been a long time since I've seen a friendly Human face."*

"Let's hope Afarra's still standing when we get there."

"Do you think Jowra will have attacked them?"

"I hope not."

"Me too."

After a whole day's reprieve from the snow, a snowstorm inevitably arrived. Huge flakes fell from the grey sky and clung stubbornly to Bandor's armour, while Oracus used more and more Larmu Ziel to keep himself warm.

For hours, the snow came, and not once did the landscape change. The north remained as white as ever, while to the rear, the trees of the Black Forest became obscured by the falling snow. Oracus remained on Bandor's back, only occasionally moving to wipe frost from his face and icicles from his hair.

"Should we stop for the night?" Oracus asked Bandor.

"If you're tired, Oracus, then go to sleep," Bandor said. *"But I'll carry on."*

"You'll be exhausted," Oracus claimed.

"I'm a Lavorian. I could do this all week," Bandor said proudly.

"I hope we're not still travelling through snow in a week, because that'll mean we're lost," Oracus joked.

Darkness came soon after, and with thick clouds covering the moon, it was impossible to see anything through Human eyes. In fact, even Bandor's incredible sight was restricted. With nothing to see, Oracus rested his head on Bandor's mane and closed his eyes, hoping sleep would come to him. But with the frost gnawing at his skin and his stash of Larmu Ziel depleted, the endless shivering kept him conscious. Occasionally, he would fall into a light snooze, but dreams of Jowra would plague his sleep and force him awake. And if it wasn't the King or his roaring Dragons, it was the battle-cries of Eeveks, Lisors and Grevlors.

When dreaming, Oracus would feel an acute rage, as if he was Jowra himself. And the frigid temperatures of the palace in Melzor were glorious. But when he awoke, he detested the frozen plains of the south, yet the anger still dwelled within him.

"Oracus, are you okay?" Bandor finally asked, drawing him out of his latest dream.

Oracus shook his head to clear his mind. *"I keep having visions of him, Bandor. I can't stop it."*

"Maybe you should stay awake for a while," Bandor proposed.

"It's since I touched the roots of Iniril. He knows now that I'm

alive, and it's like he wants me to have visions of him."

"You need to stop thinking about him, it could be dangerous."

"I'm not doing it on purpose, Bandor!" Oracus claimed, his temper rising as he spoke. He rolled from Bandor's back and kicked at the snowy ground. *"I hate that I feel this way!"*

Bandor entered Oracus's mind and growled as he took on the anger himself.

"I'm sorry," Oracus said sadly. *"I don't know what's happening to me."*

"Neither do I," Bandor replied. *"We'll have to try and understand it when we reach Afarra."*

"But we need to get there first. It could take weeks," Oracus said apprehensively. *"I can't cope with having thoughts of Jowra every time I fall asleep."*

Bandor didn't respond and Oracus felt his own concern mirrored in his Lavorian.

"I hope there's a place we can stop soon," Oracus continued, climbing back into Bandor's saddle. *"I could do with a break from the cold."*

Bandor endured through the thickening snow for the rest of the night, and Oracus fought off sleep for most of it. Occasionally, he fell into a slumber, but although Jowra still crept into his dreams, the anger wasn't quite as fierce.

When the first tendrils of daylight emerged in the morning, the land was still as white as ever: snowy ground and cloudy sky. The heavy snowfall had subsided somewhat, but it was still much colder than Oracus would have liked.

"Oracus, look!" Bandor said enthusiastically.

Oracus raised his head and looked into the distance. What looked like a city was no more than a speck on the horizon in front of them.

"Do you have any idea what that place is?" Oracus asked him.

"No," Bandor replied. *"But I doubt it's somewhere good."*

"We should head towards it," Oracus suggested. *"Maybe we can stock up on supplies there."*

"I'd say there's more chance of us being killed."

"We're stronger now than we once were," Oracus said confidently. *"We'll be fine."*

Bandor continued forwards, but during the night his eager run had reduced to a slow amble.

"Do you need to rest?" Oracus asked him.

"I can rest when we get there. Let's keep going."

For the following hours, Bandor plodded over the icy ground, persisting despite his exhaustion. Oracus occasionally dismounted his saddle to lessen the load for Bandor to carry, and he often broke the ice that was building up between the Lavorian's metal joints.

The city was drawing nearer, but not as quickly as Oracus had hoped. The longer the day went on, the more nervous he became, and the more he wished he hadn't suggested travelling there in the first place. He took a deep breath, but his heightened senses caught a whiff of something unusual in the air.

"Bandor, can you smell that?" he asked, looking around him.

Bandor raised his head and sniffed. *"Yes, I can."*

"Do you know what it is?"

"I have no idea, but it's all around us."

Oracus scanned the snow but couldn't see anything. *"Are you sure it isn't coming from that city?"*

"I'm positive," he replied. He pressed his nose against the ground and sniffed some more. *"It's coming from the snow*

itself," he deduced.

His words had barely left him when the floor around them began to shudder. The snow shifted, and before Oracus could even contemplate running, thirty short two-legged creatures climbed out of the ground and encircled them.

Oracus let out a yell of surprise. The creatures were vicious looking, their menacing, grey eyes and pointed fangs made up a narrow face without a nose. Their skin was a light shade of blue, and the hair on their heads wiry and silver. Their bodies were wrapped in rolls of white cloth dusted in the fresh snow they had been lying in, while their hands and feet were bare to the cold. Each of the creatures pointed a sharp dagger at Oracus and Bandor, of which the blade was made of ice.

"Who are you?" one of the creatures hissed unpleasantly. It was barely half Oracus's height, but it stepped forwards and waved its dagger aggressively.

"Should we fight them, Bandor?" Oracus quizzed with his mind.

"We should just see what they want," Bandor suggested.

"I doubt they want to be our friends."

"But they may not want to kill us either."

"Who are you?" the creature repeated impatiently. It bared its teeth and puffed out its little chest.

"Oracus and Bandor," Oracus said clearly. "Rider and Lavorian from the north."

"But you have come from the south," the creature retorted smartly, unfazed by Oracus declaring himself a Rider.

"We are on our way home. We have been travelling."

"Travelling where?" the creature probed.

"From Tallarin."

"Tallarin was overtaken by the King more than a year ago," the creature claimed. "And you are not one of the King's Riders."

Oracus glanced worriedly at Bandor. He had feared Tallarin's defeat but never received confirmation of it.

"Which means you either travel extremely slowly," the creature went on. "Or you are a liar."

"We spent time in the Black Forest," Bandor said.

"Nobody leaves the Black Forest alive, Lavorian," the creature replied, turning its grey eyes on Bandor.

"Well, we did."

The creature considered him. "I do not believe you. But neither do I have the authority to decide the fate of a Rider or Lavorian. You will accompany us to Malum."

Oracus's eyes widened at the name of the city. "We will *not* accom–"

"–it would be our pleasure to travel with you," Bandor interrupted.

"Very good," the creature answered. "You will walk ahead while we follow behind. And no funny business!"

Oracus turned to Bandor as the two of them began to move. *"Why did you say we would go with them?"*

"I feel more comfortable agreeing with them," Bandor explained. *"We can flee from them later if we feel we must."*

"You're too trusting. Malum is one of Jowra's cities."

"It was you who suggested we go there in the first place," Bandor countered. *"And it'll be far easier getting in with these strange looking beasts than by ourselves."*

"But I'm not sure we should go there at all now," Oracus said. *"What if Jowra is there?"*

"Jowra never leaves Melzor. So the chances of that are highly

unlikely. And I doubt whoever else lives there could challenge us now. Especially with Sarvon and Tarnu's training."

"I suppose you're right," Oracus admitted reluctantly.

Bandor winked at him. *"I always am."*

FOURTEEN

Malum

Oracus and Bandor were transported to Malum with the icy blades of thirty daggers pointed at their backs. By the time they were at the entrance to the city, night had begun to fall once more, and Oracus could no longer feel his hands or feet because of the cold.

Malum's outer-wall was tall, thick, deep blue in colour, and partially blanketed by frosty snow. The wall surrounded the entire city to make it impregnable, except for the arched entryway at the front. The archway glowed with magical light, and was secured by a heavy, ice portcullis. As the blue-skinned creatures reached the portcullis, it rose and offered passage through to the other side.

The inside of the city was dark and quiet, as if light and sound were afraid to unveil themselves. Oracus fingered the hilt of his sword and strained Bandor's senses, readying himself for an ambush that could have been waiting around any corner. The buildings were of the same magnificent blue as the surrounding wall, some with fearsome gargoyles protruding from their roofs, and others with writing and drawings carved into their walls. When the path between the buildings became especially narrow, Oracus ran his fingers along the walls. They were cold and damp; made of ice, just as he'd suspected.

The further they were taken into the city, the darker and more eerie it became, until Oracus could barely even see the path he was walking on, even with Bandor's eyesight aiding him. The shadows alongside the buildings seemed to swell and move at the sight of them, but it was impossible to see what lay within. All of a sudden, Oracus began to regret entering the city. He should have just fled from the blue creatures and continued north on Bandor's back.

"I'm sure they'd have tried to kill us already if that was their intention," Bandor said, reading Oracus's concern.

"So what do you think they want from us?" he asked.

"Maybe they want us to fight for them."

"And what happens when we say no? I doubt they'll just let us leave."

"If they try and keep us here then we'll kill them all and find our own way out."

"But we don't even know what we're up against," Oracus stated. *"Is this city full of little blue men, or is there something more sinister lurking in the shadows?"*

"You worry too much. After everything we've been through together, there's nothing we should fear–"

But Bandor was cut short as they turned a corner and Oracus felt a presence build in his mind. *"Oh no, Bandor. There's a Rider here!"* he exclaimed.

The wall of courage Bandor had been building in his mind crumbled slightly. *"A Rider?"* he repeated worriedly.

"Yes, and she's so powerful," Oracus added as the Rider's mind pushed forcefully against his own.

"A woman?" Bandor asked. He forced his way into Oracus's mind to check. *"I haven't heard anyone speak of another woman Rider in Pharia. I thought Kivali and Dyma were the only two."*

"I don't think she's Human though," Oracus said, holding his head in his hands. *"She feels... different."*

The dark, chilling passages then opened up to reveal a wide street that sparkled beneath a sky full of snow. At the end of the street, an extraordinary palace stood waiting. It was as icy as the rest of the city, but exploding with white light that lit up everything around it. From its pointy spires to the grand steps at its base, it had been as finely crafted as any of the other palaces Oracus had seen in Pharia. In fact, Oracus wondered if it might have been the finest of them all.

As the blue-skinned creatures led Oracus and Bandor towards the palace, the unknown Rider's mind built in strength. The fear Oracus began to feel brought him to a halt, but a small hand pressed into his back, and an impatient voice rasped at him, "Keep moving!"

They ascended the icy steps and were met by a set of doors that creaked into life as they approached. The light that came from beyond was blinding, and Oracus covered his eyes with his hand. Another push in the back forced him onwards.

They came to a foyer where fifty more of the same creatures waited in a line, their icy daggers raised threateningly. Like the creatures that had marched Oracus and Bandor into the palace, these were indistinguishable from one another, short in stature with fierce faces and sharp fangs. The foyer itself was vast in size and freezing in temperature, affording Oracus no relief from the cold outside. The ice pillars holding up the ceiling were carved magnificently, and the walls were decorated with cleverly crafted patterns of white frost. There were arched openings all around the walls too, and Oracus and Bandor were led through the grandest of them all, into a spectacular chamber where the power of the Rider's mind almost knocked Oracus off balance.

As the blue-skinned creatures dispersed to adopt their positions by the icy walls, Oracus was left standing alone with Bandor in a scenario that so closely resembled his first meeting with Torvanon in Afarra. Beneath his feet, a long silver rug had been laid out along the centre of the room, and at the other end of the rug, a platform two steps high was occupied by a Rider upon an ice throne, alongside her giant Polar-Bear Lavorian. From within the icy walls and ceiling, magical light shone upon the pair, causing the throne to glisten and the silver armour of the Lavorian to appear white.

Oracus gulped as the fear took hold of him. Never had he expected to find such a powerful Rider and Lavorian here – although it should have been obvious to him that Jowra wouldn't leave one of his most valued cities under the protection of weaker men.

Oracus wondered how long he and Bandor would survive, for there was no chance of Bandor defeating the Polar-Bear. It was far too big. *"Why did we think it would be safe to come here?"* he whispered inside Bandor's mind. *"We'll never make it out this palace alive, let alone the city."*

With his eyes still on the throne, Oracus thought furiously about how they might escape. That was until the Rider looked at him and his breath was taken away. From outside the palace, Oracus had thought this Rider wasn't

Human, but in fact, she was the most beautiful Human he had ever seen.

When her eyes met his, the woman stared momentarily, perhaps startled by the unexpected appearance of a Rider and Lavorian in her palace. But she quickly gathered herself, and a wide smile soon came to her lips. "Welcome to Malum!" she announced, and she raised her arms invitingly. "What an honour it is to have you both here."

Oracus hadn't anticipated such a friendly greeting, and he could only find a blank expression to respond with.

"And your names?" the woman prompted, rising gracefully from her seat.

"Oracus and Bandor, Your Highness," Oracus stuttered, struggling to make his voice work properly. He did offer a bow though, for he wasn't sure how she should be addressed.

"Your Highness?" the woman repeated with a smirk. "You flatter me, Oracus. I am no Queen or Princess. I just happen to own a throne."

The woman began to walk forwards with both grace and purpose, and Oracus couldn't take his eyes off her. After she descended the steps from the platform, he realised she was slightly taller than him, with legs that never seemed to end. She was blonde, with wavy hair that fell beyond her shoulders and swayed gently with each of her strides. She had alluring blue eyes that glistened like icicles, and skin as smooth as the ice walls all around.

When she reached Oracus, she smiled again, and he realised his mouth was hanging open. She wore a grey dress that matched the colour of the rug beneath their feet, and a corset underneath that revealed every curve of her body. A white fur robe hung from her shoulders and glided along the floor behind her.

"You're a very handsome young man," she offered coquettishly. As she said it, she raised her hand to touch Oracus's cheek and he flushed violently. The woman laughed, and Oracus saw her teeth were as white as snow.

"So, what brings you to my city?" she added.

Oracus gulped to wet his throat. "We were just passing by," he croaked.

"Well I'm glad my friends here convinced you to come." She waved a hand at the blue-skinned creatures nearby. "It would have been a shame to miss you."

"What are the creatures called?" Bandor asked. Oracus could feel in his mind that the Lion was keen to speak to this incredible lady.

"They are Azzeils from the Sirin Mountains," the woman answered. "I invited them here when I built this city."

"You built this whole city yourself?" Bandor asked.

"With a little help from the Azzeils, of course." The woman stepped towards Bandor and ran her hand softly over his mane. Then she scratched his chin. "You are quite magnificent, Bandor. Possibly the finest Lavorian I have ever seen."

Bandor purred and Oracus scowled, jealous that the Lion's chin was being scratched and not his.

"I quite like her," Bandor said.

"I can see that," Oracus replied, scowling all the more.

"My name is Xintora," the woman continued. "And my Lavorian here is Jhaqar." She pointed up at the Polar-Bear that still stood on the platform. Its big black eyes had been studying Oracus and Bandor closely since their arrival.

"It's nice to meet you both," Oracus said. He found himself nodding at Jhaqar, hoping to gain the approval of the colossal Lavorian. But his nod wasn't returned.

"You look cold and malnourished," Xintora observed, standing back and looking Oracus up and down.

"We've been travelling in the snow for over a day," Bandor explained.

"And where have you travelled from?" Jhaqar asked. His sudden booming voice made Oracus jump, and its echo made white frost sprinkle down from the ceiling. The Lavorian walked slowly forwards, scraping his metal claws over the ice. With each step, the floor trembled under his weight.

"We found ourselves in the Black Forest after leaving Tallarin. And from there we travelled here." Oracus looked up at Jhaqar as he spoke and felt extremely intimidated.

Neither Jhaqar nor Xintora replied for a moment and Oracus suspected they were communicating with their minds.

"The Azzeils didn't believe us either," Oracus said.

"We didn't say we don't believe you," Jhaqar said. "But how did you escape the forest?"

Oracus glanced at Bandor and then looked back at Jhaqar. "The Ulatoris released us," he answered.

"That is unusual of the Ulatoris. They would normally kill trespassers," Xintora said. "What reason did they give for letting you go?"

"We have agreed to return something of theirs," Bandor said.

"And what something would that be?"

"The Ulatori traitor, Gravaz," Oracus said.

Xintora and Jhaqar *definitely* shared a thought on that occasion. They were silent for almost thirty seconds, and both of them failed to hide their shock.

"How do you expect to do that?" Xintora asked finally. "Gravaz lives in the northernmost city of Pharia, and he's a very powerful Rider."

"We haven't planned that far ahead yet," Oracus replied.

Xintora raised a thin eyebrow, intrigued. "Are you aware he's one of King Jowra's servants?"

"We know that, yes," Bandor said.

"Yet you still wish to capture him and deliver him to the Ulatoris in the Black Forest?" Xintora's eyes were fixed on Oracus. She appeared amused, but curious. "Not only is it dangerous, but it's also treachery against the King."

Oracus considered his next words carefully. Xintora seemed friendly, but he didn't yet trust her enough to admit treason. "This place is called Malum, right?" he asked. "It's one of Jowra's cities."

"That's correct," Xintora granted.

"Then don't you answer to him just as Gravaz does? I think I've already said too much by admitting my plans for Gravaz," Oracus said.

An entertained look crossed Xintora's face. "Do I look like the kind of woman to go running to the King with secrets at every given opportunity?"

"I don't know," Oracus said truthfully.

Xintora tutted impatiently. "I am not bound to the King. A friend of his is not necessarily a friend of mine. Just as an enemy of his is not necessarily an enemy of mine."

"So you'll keep my plans a secret from him then?"

"The weaker the King becomes, the closer I get to ruling this city without him watching over my shoulder. I will not speak of you or your plans to him, for doing so is not in my best interests."

Oracus nodded appreciatively, but still wasn't convinced

by her words. His first impression was that she was beautiful, elegant and kind, but something about her made him feel uncomfortable. Maybe it was the giant Polar-Bear Lavorian at her side, or the vicious Azzeils that worked for her. Or perhaps Oracus struggled to trust anyone who chose to live in a palace made of ice.

"We should get you both some food," Xintora said, changing the route of the conversation. She was still scrutinising Oracus, and it made him wonder whether his admissions to her had been wise. "Come with me."

Oracus and Bandor turned as Xintora glided between them and headed towards the foyer from where they had entered. Jhaqar and the blue creatures remained in the chamber, leaving Xintora to lead them through the palace alone. In the foyer, they passed through a frozen archway that led to a different area of the palace, then they advanced along a corridor and up a staircase. The emptiness of it all was quite eerie, and the abundance of blue ice and biting cold gave Oracus the sensation of being underwater. Perhaps this was what it felt like to be a fish.

Eventually, Xintora led them into a small, square room. The walls and ceiling were bare, but in the centre of the room was an ice table with plates of juicy meats and vegetables full of colour. There were bowls of bread and fruit too, and goblets of wine scattered throughout. The sight made Oracus's stomach rumble, and he was suddenly very aware of how hungry he was.

Xintora seated herself at the head of the table and pointed at another chair for Oracus to take. "Make yourself comfortable," she offered. "Indulge."

Oracus didn't need telling twice. He sat and zestfully plucked food from the crockery, filling his mouth with whatever would fit in it. Occasionally he would wash it down with a gulp of fruity wine before eagerly cramming more food into his mouth.

"You look like you're enjoying yourself," Bandor said in his mind.

"I am," Oracus replied. *"This food is to die for."*

"Well, hopefully we don't actually die for it."

Xintora herself didn't eat, but she watched Oracus ardently. With each mouthful he consumed, her polished smile grew a little wider, and her deep blue eyes gleamed a little more.

"This is really tasty," Oracus said each time he spotted her studying him.

"You are so kind," was always her response. Every time, her long eyelashes would flutter at him flirtatiously.

Oracus ate until he felt on the cusp of sickness. When he was done, he leaned back and held his belly in his hands.

"Are you finished?" Xintora asked him.

Oracus nodded and let out a sigh of fulfilment. He was so full that he thought he might burst.

"Good. Because I was hoping I could ask you more questions."

Oracus was now so content that Xintora no longer intimidated him. Especially now she was separated from Jhaqar. "Ask away," he said.

"Where in Pharia you are from?"

"A little village in the Raspian Forest to the north," Oracus answered.

"Are the people of the Raspian Forest trustworthy?" Xintora asked.

"I would consider myself trustworthy, but I can't speak for everyone else who lives there," Oracus claimed.

"Then help me to trust you by telling me what your power is," Xintora said.

The abruptness of the question shocked Oracus, and he felt uneasiness creep into his mind from Bandor.

"Don't answer that," his Lavorian advised. *"We don't want her to know you're a Vassath."*

"I don't know what my power is yet," Oracus lied cleverly.

"You don't?" Xintora asked, surprised. Her eyes bored into his own and he was sure she didn't believe him. "But how long ago was it that you two bonded?"

"Only a few months," Oracus answered, trying his best not to look away from her challenging stare.

Xintora stood up and glided towards Bandor with her fur robe dragging along the floor behind her. "Yet your Lavorian is so big and strong," she said. She ran her fingers through his mane and Bandor shivered with pleasure. "How can you not know your power, Oracus?"

"I just don't," he replied, but he didn't sound convincing.

"Oh well. I guess it's just one of those things," Xintora said after a moment's pause. Her stern expression eased. "Now tell me how long you're thinking of staying here?"

"Do you have a room free for the night?" Oracus asked, relieved that the topic of conversation had changed. "It would be nice to rest before we continue our journey tomorrow."

"Just one night?" Xintora replied, somewhat disappointedly.

"I need to get back home," Oracus said. "And I don't want to be in the cold for longer than necessary."

"I understand. But you are welcome to stay longer if you change your mind," she said kindly. She then clapped her hands together and two Azzeil guards came into the room with their ice daggers drawn. "Take this handsome pair upstairs and show them where they'll be sleeping," she ordered. She offered Oracus and Bandor one final alluring smile. "Make sure you sleep well. I want you fresh for breakfast in the morning."

FIFTEEN

Ice Prison

The room they were granted for the night was as bitterly cold as the rest of the palace, and Oracus lay on an ice bed watching his misty breath rise towards the ceiling. He shivered as he thought about how alone he and Bandor were, and how vulnerable they were as a result. Although Xintora appeared charming, she ruled one of Jowra's cities and commanded a huge Lavorian. So it was little surprise that Oracus suspected something underhand was at play.

But notwithstanding all these concerns, Oracus had one reason to be glad of Xintora's presence. Her mind was so potent that he could easily discern her power, even though she was elsewhere in the palace. She was an ice conjurer, and she could shoot ice from her hands like Gravaz could throw balls of fire from his. Silently, Oracus thanked Sarvon for training him to understand and refine his power. He then connected to Xintora's mind and a jet of ice erupted from his palm and smashed into the wall of the room.

Having been asleep, Bandor almost leapt out his armour in fright, and Oracus couldn't help but laugh.

"Why would you do that?" the Lion said unhappily.

"Sorry, I should have warned you," Oracus replied. Then he enthusiastically cast more ice around the room.

It wasn't until the early hours of the morning that the novelty of his new power wore off. And even then Oracus wasn't sleepy. There were too many worries floating around in his head. His biggest worry of all was dreaming about Jowra as soon as he closed his eyes, but he also found himself thinking of his parents, his friends in Afarra, and his promise to Sarvon. Then there was Xintora herself; with her flowing blonde hair, her dazzling blue eyes, her pearly white smile, her fluttering eyelashes, her tight corset…

Oracus shook the thought from his head and cursed at himself. *"I can't sleep, Bandor,"* he said, sitting up. *"I'm going to have a look around."*

"Are you sure that's a good idea?" Bandor replied as he stirred, for he'd had no problem sleeping.

"I feel like something odd is going on here and I'm keen to investigate. Don't worry, I won't leave the palace."

Oracus swung his legs off the bed and stood. He fastened his dagger to his belt before ruffling Bandor's mane and heading to the door. Pushing it open, he scanned the corridor outside, only to see the magical lights in the walls illuminating the way. He proceeded cautiously, careful not to make too much noise, until he reached a spiral staircase at the end of the corridor.

Realising he'd been holding his breath, he gasped, then he started to descend the steps, believing that down was safer than up.

Oracus's fear built the further down he climbed, and he counted himself lucky that he didn't encounter a single guard. It was only when he reached the bottom of the staircase that any sign of life revealed itself. There was a loud clang from somewhere nearby and Oracus spotted the silhouette of a lone Azzeil as he peeked around the corner. It was particularly dark and cold down here, and Oracus presumed he was in a basement beneath the palace.

The Azzeil walked along a passage and through a doorway, and Oracus followed quietly at a distance. He could still feel Xintora's mind, so was comfortable knowing he could use her power should he need to, but it was his preference to keep his presence a secret. The last thing he wanted was for Xintora to find out he'd been sneaking around in her palace.

At the doorway where the Azzeil had disappeared, Oracus waited out of sight and listened for any sign the creature was standing on the other side. When he was sure it was safe, he advanced through the door and found himself facing a sight that shocked him to the core. What he had expected to be another narrow passage turned out to be a chamber as vast as it was magnificent. It was a prison on a scale Oracus had never even dreamt of. It was so large he couldn't see where it ended, and there were cells every two strides with thick icicles acting as a door to each. Separating the cells on the left from those on the right was a deep gorge in the ice. Edging forwards, Oracus looked into the gorge and realised he was on the topmost of a dozen floors that all held as many cells as each other. From somewhere down below, he heard a scream, and then the sound of someone being beaten.

Oracus backed away in horror. This was not at all what he expected to find. He looked around to check for guards, but instead spotted a prisoner in the nearest cell. The occupant was a Human with straggly grey hair and deep wrinkled skin. He wore only a tattered burlap sack, and was sat in the corner of the cell with his knees tucked under his chin, trying to keep himself warm. But his blotchy purple skin gave away just how cold he was. He looked so cold in fact, Oracus was unsure how the man was still alive.

At the sight of Oracus, the old man lifted his head and reached out a hopeful, trembling hand. "Help me," he mouthed, but no sound came out.

"Bandor, wake up," Oracus ordered.

"What? Are you in danger?" came Bandor's worried reply.

"No, but you need to see this."

Oracus felt Bandor probing his mind. Then the Lion was in his head, scanning the prison through his eyes.

"It's a prison under the palace," Oracus explained while Bandor looked around.

"Are all the prisoners Humans?" Bandor asked.

Oracus walked past the cells, glancing into each one and seeing old men and women curled up in a corner, just like the man in the first cell had been. They were all purple from cold and appeared to be on the brink of death.

"Every one looks Human," Oracus replied, sickened. *"Why do you think they're here?"*

Bandor was quiet for a moment while Oracus passed more cells. *"I think we've been lied to, Oracus,"* he said finally. *"These must be Jowra's captives and Xintora is guarding them for him."*

Oracus suddenly felt himself go very cold; colder than usual in this frozen palace. And that's when it happened.

An agony coursed through his body so severe he was sure it would shatter his bones. He fell to his knees and screamed at the height of his voice, unable to withstand the pain. He knew what was coming, for this kind of pain he only ever experienced during the most vivid of dreams. The first time had been when his mother appeared in the Raspian Forest on the night he bonded with Bandor. And the second time was in Lalacia's library when King Xarmoud had revealed himself. These dreams were never actually dreams, they were visions, and they always tore Oracus away from reality.

The pain eased as abruptly as it had begun, and Oracus was able to open his eyes. But no longer did he find himself in the icy prison of Malum. He was in Melzor with the man he hated more than any other: Jowra.

*

Jowra felt the skin on his palms prickle; the first sign that one of his many spies was in distress. He walked through the dimly lit corridors that snaked through his palace and headed down to the keep where his Dragons slept. All the while, he scratched his palms with his long fingernails, desperate for the prickle to subside.

When he reached the keep, Jowra pushed the doors open wide, then raised himself off the ground and glided towards where his Dragons were stirring. The cold air from the open sky whipped his black hair across his face and he shivered with pleasure. Then he landed upon a ridge in Wravias's neck. It was a private place where he could concentrate without interruption.

"What is the matter, Xintora?" he asked as he entered the mind of his distant servant.

"He's here in Malum, my King," Xintora replied.

"Who is there?"

"The Rider from Tallarin. The boy Gravaz claimed was dead," she said. *"He's here in the palace."*

A thrill pulsed through Jowra's mind and he sensed Xintora's discomfort as she felt it herself. *"What have you done with him?"* Jowra asked.

"He's sleeping in one of the rooms," Xintora answered.

"Have you not detained him?"

"I haven't needed to, my King," she said. *"I've been very warm towards him. He doesn't suspect a thing."*

"You must detain him now!" Jowra demanded. *"Before he gets away."*

"Don't worry, my King, he's trapped here. He can't get away."

"I don't care what you think he can or cannot do, Xintora! This boy has been a burden of mine for far too long! Imprison him yourself immediately. Then tell me when it is done."

"Yes, my King. I'll do it right away."

Jowra released himself from Xintora's mind. He watched Wravias and Pseubas snap playfully at each other for a moment, then returned to his thoughts. He had hoped Gravaz's words were true and that the boy was dead, but it appeared Gravaz was a liar. Suddenly, there was an anxiety building within Jowra. This boy had escaped his grasp twice before; once in Fervia and then in Tallarin too. He couldn't afford for him to escape a third time. But Jowra would have to rely on one of his servants once again, and that was infuriating. If he was in Malum himself then he would ensure the boy met his end, but there was no way he would risk leaving the safety of his palace in Melzor after everything he had built.

Jowra cursed and raised himself from Wravias's neck. He glided carefully back to the floor of the keep and then began to pace back and forth. He was desperate for Xintora to succeed, and he hoped she would prove herself to him more than Gravaz and Zarad had done. But he doubted it. There was only one person he could trust, and that was himself.

*

The dream dispersed as quickly as the pain had. Oracus came around and found himself in the icy prison once more, lying face down on the cold floor. But no longer was it quiet and calm like before. Now there was pandemonium.

Hundreds of Azzeils had appeared where there had previously been none. Many were investigating cells and checking the prisoners were still inside, whilst others were hissing commands to each other in a language Oracus didn't understand.

Oracus kept still and spoke privately to Bandor. *"I've had a vision,"* he said. *"Xintora works for Jowra. She told him we're here."*

"I know, I saw everything," Bandor replied. *"I was still in your head when you were dreaming."*

"So what do we do now?" Oracus asked as the panic began to set in.

"How quickly can you get back to the room?" Bandor returned.

"Fairly quickly so long as I can get past these Azzeils."

"Then hurry!"

Oracus felt his emotions drain and his senses intensify as Bandor delved into his mind. When he lifted his head, the Azzeils that had been stepping over his body recoiled in terror before pointing their daggers at him.

It felt like time had slowed down as he rose to his feet. All around him the Azzeils came to a halt until he felt he was at the centre of an entire army. Individually, he did not fear the creatures, for they were only half his height. But faced with a legion, it was an intimidating scenario.

"You shouldn't be down here," one of the Azzeils shouted angrily. "You are trespassing!"

Another then made himself heard above the crowd, "We should kill him and deliver his body to Xintora!"

The Azzeils all took a step forward as one and Oracus knew he would have to fight to escape. Yet there were so many of them, and they were blocking the exit too.

"Use Xintora's power," Bandor prompted.

Oracus didn't need to be told twice. He dropped to his knees, extended both hands, then swivelled as he shot a continuous stream of ice at every Azzeil that had trapped him. Most of the closest creatures took ice to the face and were knocked backwards and sideways, while others tumbled under the weight of their comrades. Oracus hadn't expected his power to come with such force, and some of the Azzeils fell down the gorge, never to be seen again.

With his enemies stunned, Oracus made a dash for the exit and soon found himself in the passage that led to the spiral staircase. He turned back and fired ice at the doorway, blocking it to stop any Azzeils following him. But before he could take to the stairs, he heard the patter of many small feet coming down. Knowing he was soon to be confronted by another horde, he sprayed the bottom steps with ice. Without his sword, he was vulnerable, so he needed every advantage he could get.

He stepped back and clenched his fists, then waited for the Azzeils to arrive. The first of them hit the slippery steps and tumbled helplessly, then a dozen more followed suit. Oracus jumped over the building pile of Azzeils, punched his way through the stragglers who hadn't fallen, and then ascended the staircase alone, satisfied with how well his plan had worked.

At the top of the stairs, Oracus became very aware of Xintora's mind. It was becoming stronger, which meant she was getting closer to him. He picked up his speed and ran to the room where Bandor was waiting.

"She's coming!" he exclaimed worriedly as he crashed through the door.

Bandor was stood ready, his saddle still strapped to him from the day before. *"Don your armour and grab your sword,"* he advised.

Oracus did as he was told, but he was still pulling his chestplate over his head when the door to their quarters was blown apart. Shards of ice scattered across the floor as Xintora stepped through the hole she had created.

"Climb on now!" Bandor commanded.

Oracus snatched his sword from the floor and jumped into Bandor's saddle. The Lion turned as Xintora threw her first ball of ice, then he reared as the second ball struck his side.

"There's nowhere to run," Xintora claimed triumphantly. *"Surrender to me."*

With a defiant roar, Bandor charged at the wall behind them and burst through the thick ice. Even Oracus hadn't expected his Lavorian to attempt such an outrageous escape, and he cried out as they plummeted several storeys. When they hit the ground, the ice cracked all around them and Oracus was thrown from Bandor's back. Oracus heard some nearby Azzeil guards shriek with fright as they appeared, then he dragged himself to his feet, amazed he hadn't broken a bone.

"You're crazy," he said, shaking his head.

"I don't think there was another choice," the Lavorian responded.

Looking back up at the palace, Oracus saw Xintora glaring down at them from the hole they'd just made in her beautiful palace. She was incensed, and her hair was wild too – it was quite the contrast from her warmth the evening before. She fired several inaccurate jets of ice from her viewpoint and Oracus climbed back into Bandor's saddle.

"We need to get out of here," he said with urgency. *"Before she comes after us."*

The Azzeil guards kept at a distance, evidently unwilling to fight a Rider and Lavorian who had dropped from the sky. They looked furious; their fangs bared just like their ice daggers.

"Do you know the way out the city?" Oracus questioned his Lavorian.

"I don't remember the exact route to the gate, but if we just go straight then we'll eventually reach the outer wall," Bandor suggested.

"Good idea," Oracus agreed.

They set off at a gallop, desperate to get as far away from Xintora as possible. But the relief of escaping the palace was short-lived. Where Oracus had expected to feel the intensity of Xintora's mind dwindle, it actually began to build. And with it came several violent quakes of the ground.

"Can you feel that, Bandor?" he questioned with concern.

"I think there might be a Polar-Bear chasing us," Bandor answered.

Oracus swivelled in his seat to check their rear. *"But I don't see anyth–"*

As he spoke, a tall building they'd just passed crumbled. From behind it, Jhaqar arrived at speed, his giant frame demolishing everything in his path.

Oracus had never felt such fear. Even with Bandor at full speed, Jhaqar was gaining on them easily, and it wasn't long before the Polar-Bear's head was looming over them. Now that Jhaqar was so close, Oracus could see Xintora stood upon his back. But no longer was she the alluring woman from the palace. Instead, Oracus found himself staring at a creature that barely resembled a Human. Her skin was now green and scaly, with a face full of venom and three thin tails whipping the air behind her. Her hands had been replaced with sharp claws too, and she held a spectacular trident above her head.

Just as Oracus had thought when he first entered Malum, Xintora wasn't Human. She was a hideous beast with the ability to change her appearance. He reflected on his conversation with her in her throne room and wondered why he had been so quick to believe her. Just as she had hidden her true physical form, she had hidden her loyalty to Jowra.

Bandor danced gracefully between the buildings as Jhaqar crushed everything in his pursuit of them. And balls of ice flashed by Oracus and exploded on the ground as Xintora aimed to unseat him. The further they travelled, the more deafening Jhaqar's footfall became. The sound of metal on ice was horribly piercing, and it made Oracus wince with every step.

"I can see the wall, Oracus!" Bandor exclaimed suddenly, pulling Oracus's attention away from the enemy. *"But I don't know how we can get through it with Jhaqar so close."*

Oracus spotted the wall himself. It was a fair distance away still, but the path to it was straight and empty. He managed to throw an iceball of his own over his shoulder as he considered his and Bandor's options, but it smashed unnoticed against Jhaqar's armour.

"I have an idea," he said after a moment. *"I need you to take away all my emotions and keep running at that wall."*

Bandor was more than willing to oblige and Oracus felt his fear dissipate immediately. He launched several more iceballs at their pursuers before the wall was only one-hundred strides away. Then he focused his power on the ground before them and started creating a path of ice that rose gradually upwards.

"Start climbing, Bandor!" he yelled.

Bandor's paws hit the new path and the top of the wall came swiftly nearer. But the closer their escape came, the more Oracus could feel Jhaqar's hot breath on the back of his neck. Even with Bandor soaking up his feelings, Oracus was apprehensive. But he didn't dare focus on anything other than the icy path he was creating. For they were only metres from the wall now. Just half a dozen strides away…

"Jump, Bandor!" Oracus cried.

Oracus's insides somersaulted as Bandor leapt. He looked down as they soared over the gap between path and wall, and all his emotions came flooding back. Fear consumed him, and all he could think to do was throw a final ball of ice at Xintora.

Fortunately, his aim was true. As Jhaqar lunged forwards and prepared to snatch Oracus and Bandor out the air, the ice struck Xintora's midriff and flung her backwards. Jhaqar had no choice but to abandon his prey and save his own Rider, and Oracus and Bandor successfully landed on the other side of the wall.

There was a moment of concern for Oracus, for he knew Jhaqar may skid through Malum's outer wall. But after a resounding thump and a gentle quake in the ground, the wall stood firm, and Oracus pumped his fists in celebration.

"We did it!" he yelled. "We escaped!"

Bandor was panting, and Oracus could sense his relief. But there was a measure of regret in the Lavorian's mind too.

"Is everything okay?" Oracus asked him.

"We got out, but all those prisoners are still in there," Bandor replied. "I wish we could have saved them."

Oracus's excitement faded as the memory of the old man in the prison came back to him. What stuck with him most was the desperation he'd seen in the man's eyes.

"There's no way we could have got them out of there," Oracus said truthfully. *"We barely survived by ourselves."*

"I know. I just feel terrible for leaving them though."

Silence crept over them for a few seconds as they thought about what they'd left behind. Then a growl from inside the city brought them back to reality.

"We should get away from here before they get out and follow us," Bandor suggested.

Oracus scanned the land to the north and saw a river through the falling snow. But beyond the river, he was surprised to see a land where sunshine lay in wait, with a healthy patch of trees standing green and welcoming.

"We need to get across the river," Oracus said. *"Those trees are the perfect place to hide."*

Bandor agreed, and together they crossed the last of the snowy land. It was a relief to be leaving the cold, and a relief too that they'd escaped Malum. But the relief was dampened knowing they had left behind thousands of helpless captives who would freeze in the chamber beneath the palace.

SIXTEEN

Hiding An Army

Time gradually slowed down as they neared Fervia. Three-thousand footsteps echoed loudly through the trees of the Raspian Forest as the Afarran army progressed for the fourth successive day.

Afarra had been left with limited defences; Dyma and Huadlan the only Rider and Lavorian remaining in the city. Meanwhile, scouts had been sent to Melzor to monitor movements of Jowra's army. If there was any indication that he was preparing to attack Afarra, the Afarran soldiers would abandon their advance on Fervia and return home.

Garrin, Kivali and Torvanon were the Riders leading the army to battle. They all rode upon their Lavorians – Aquila, Onca and Ursus – while Torvanon's gruff second-in-command Horvos trudged along beside them, barking orders at the men to their rear. Horvos wore armour the same shade of silver as a Lavorian's, while Garrin, Kivali and Torvanon wore green, blue and gold respectively, not that it was distinguishable to the Human eye in the darkness. The soldiers behind them wore green or blue armour, depending on whether they were from Afarra or Tallarin. But no matter their birthplace, every man carried himself with courage and purpose. Together, they believed they could bring about Jowra's downfall. And why wouldn't they with three Riders keeping them safe?

Personally, Garrin was sure their numbers would provide enough force to defeat Fervia, especially with Torvanon in their midst. But he also knew that many of the fighters wouldn't make it home alive – and there was no guarantee he would either.

"You look troubled," Torvanon observed, his deep voice creeping up on Garrin in the dark.

"I am," Garrin admitted.

"For any particular reason?"

"I might be dead soon."

Torvanon's auburn beard twitched. "You said yourself that their defences are weak – a few Humans and Grevlors patrolling the walls and manning the parapets is barely worth having. And as soon as we're in the city, their men won't have the strength to resist us. We'll be victorious in no time and returning home with smiles on our faces."

"It's the Riders that worry me, Torvanon, not the men under their command. Gravaz and Zarad aren't weak, especially with Lapsin and Mammat protecting them."

"Neither are you," Torvanon offered with a wink. "And you have Aquila."

"I wouldn't want Aquila to fight Mammat though. She wouldn't stand a chance."

"I'm more than capable of handling Mammat, thank you," Aquila stated aloud.

"Have you forgotten what happened in Alvoria?" Garrin reminded. "We were lucky to survive."

"*You* were lucky that I had your back!" Aquila exclaimed. "Mammat is big and slow; an easy target."

"It sounds like you have nothing to worry about, Garrin," Torvanon said with a chuckle. "Why don't you both take a ride. Fervia can't be too far away now and it'll be good for you to stretch your wings before we get there."

Garrin waited until they came to a clearing before taking Torvanon's advice. With an opening in the canopy, they were able to ascend towards the starry sky above.

"I didn't mean to call you incompetent," Garrin said as Aquila beat her wings to get them higher. *"I'm just concerned."*

"We'll be okay as long as we stay together," she replied seriously.

"I feel like everything is relying on us succeeding here. If we make a mistake then Jowra will be victorious."

"Then we won't make a mistake," Aquila responded.

Garrin was grateful for Aquila's optimism, but it still didn't fill him with belief. Even if Fervia *was* easy to conquer, it didn't mean Jowra would suddenly become powerless. Another of his armies would have to be defeated soon after, and that meant an attack on Melzor would need to be planned. And they would need a huge slice of good fortune to destroy a city where the King himself would be fighting.

"You're looking too far ahead," Aquila said to him after reading his thoughts. *"One step at a time."*

Ahead, Garrin spotted smoke rising into the night from an open orange fire. The scent of the fire struck him soon after, and he soaked up the last of his freedom above the trees.

"That's Fervia," he pointed out to Aquila. *"We should turn back and warn Torvanon. It's only another hour's march for the soldiers."*

Within twenty minutes, three-thousand men had made camp, and there was an anxious silence among them. The attack on Fervia was to wait until sunrise, giving the men chance to rest from their long journey.

Every soldier lay on the hard forest floor, but little sleep was had. No fires or conversations were allowed in case their position was compromised, so most men stared into the darkness, worrying about what was to come in the morning. Fortunately for Garrin, nobody could hear him or Aquila speaking to one another, so they happily chatted in silence.

"Do you know what day it is tomorrow?" Aquila asked him. *"It's three years since we bonded."*

"Already?" Garrin said, shocked.

"It's gone quickly, hasn't it?"

"Too quickly," Garrin agreed. *"But look how far we've come. We're helping lead an army into battle."*

"I'm surprised you aren't still sneaking me around your parents' house in Thessley," Aquila joked. *"Perhaps they still wouldn't have noticed I was there."*

"You're bigger than that house now," Garrin reminisced with a smile.

"And I still have plenty of growing left to do," Aquila reminded him proudly.

"I'll only be worried when you're the size of Mammat. When you're that big, there's a risk you'll stand on me by mistake."

Garrin rolled over and looked around. There were slithers of silver on the ground where the moonlight shone through the leaves, and the odd glimmer of a chestplate or sword that caught the light. The buzz of crickets was ferocious, and the occasional hoot of an owl echoed from somewhere above. But most evident were the snores of those men who had found sleep, and the snapping of twigs as soldiers fidgeted.

"I've never seen Torvanon outside Afarra's walls before," Garrin said.

"I've never heard him speak of any battles he's fought in either," Aquila added. *"I wonder how strong his power really is."*

"I don't know," Garrin mused. *"But I think he holds back when I spar with him."*

"And he has Ursus with him here too. He's a huge Lavorian, so it makes Torvanon even more powerful."

Garrin found himself wondering whether Torvanon and Ursus would be able to take down Mammat between them, for the Elephant was truly enormous.

"Do you think we'll invade more of Jowra's cities after this one?" Garrin asked.

"What do you mean?" Aquila said.

"Well, I keep wondering whether we'll need to plan another attack. When Jowra hears of Fervia's defeat, he might retaliate immediately."

"And send his army to Afarra?"

"Yes," Garrin answered.

"So long as he doesn't join the attack himself, we'll be fine."

"That's just it. We'll have to fight him at some point anyway. Whether that's because he's flown to Afarra or because we've launched an assault on Melzor." Garrin scratched his head and frowned. *"People say he's invincible. So does it really matter when we fight him? Even alone he would destroy us all."*

"Miracles can happen, so we should keep on doing what we're doing. And the imminent task is to successfully invade Fervia."

Garrin turned onto his back and looked up at the forest ceiling above. Through the leaves, he could see some stars twinkling in the sky. *"What I would do for a peaceful life right now,"* he said.

"Peace would be boring," Aquila said seriously. *"What would you need a Lavorian for without war?"*

"That's very true. I'd have to sell you at the market."

Aquila scowled. *"You wouldn't sell me!"*

"I would if someone offered the right price," he said with a sly grin.

SEVENTEEN

Battle Of Fervia

The morning brought with it heavy rain and chilling winds that whistled loudly through the trees. The weather in the north was usually warm and dry, but today it seemed to know a battle was looming and that death approached. Although the torrents and gales dampened the spirits of the soldiers, it pleased Garrin, for it would conceal the sound of their surprise attack.

Within the outermost trees of the forest, Garrin stood with Torvanon, Horvos and Kivali, peering at the wall of Fervia. It was guarded by small Human and Grevlor patrols, just as it had been on his and Aquila's scouting mission.

"I have sour memories of this city," Kivali stated, staring at the smoke rising from somewhere inside.

"Then let us hope your memories of today will be fonder," Horvos replied.

"How will we breach the walls?" Garrin asked quietly, watching a group of Grevlor guards skulk past their watch point.

"Through the front gate," Torvanon said simply.

"I doubt they'll just invite us in."

"No, but you and Kivali will distract them," Torvanon explained. "If you fly over the wall with Aquila and Kivali teleports through with Onca, you'll attract the guards and allow Horvos and I time to infiltrate."

"It sounds dangerous," Garrin said.

"I need you to keep them occupied long enough that we can start the invasion. We have three-thousand men to lead inside the walls," Torvanon said. "But if you're compromised by Gravaz or Zarad, then you both get out of there immediately. I don't want two dead Riders before the battle has even begun."

Garrin and Kivali nodded in unison before rushing back into the forest where Aquila and Onca were waiting with the army.

"I'm sorry about what happened, Garrin," Kivali said as they hurdled a fallen tree. "My head hasn't been in a good place for weeks now and I'm treating people with less respect than I usually would. You took the brunt of that when we sparred."

"It's fine," Garrin replied. He hadn't forgiven Kivali yet, but he was putting aside his feelings until after the attack on Fervia.

Kivali grabbed his hand and pulled him to a stop. "No, it isn't fine," she said strongly. "I could have hurt you, and I want to apologise for it."

"It isn't what you did to me that I'm upset about," Garrin responded. "I'm upset because you don't realise how wrong you are about Oracus. He's a good man, Kivali, not a servant of the King."

Kivali looked put out. "I still have a lot of thinking to do about that," she said.

They continued through the damp undergrowth until

they reached their two Lavorians. Garrin now felt more anxious given Kivali's poor apology.

"It's starting," Garrin said with his mind as he reached the Eagle. *"Get yourself ready for battle."*

"What has Torvanon asked you to do?" she asked.

"We're the bait."

Kivali was already astride Onca when Garrin mounted Aquila. "We'll meet you inside the city," she said.

"Sure," Garrin agreed. *"Aquila, up!"*

The rain stung Garrin's face as he and Aquila ascended into the sky. When they were high enough, Garrin could see Fervia clearly over the treetops. It was a quarter the size of Afarra, but the stone buildings had been built tall and strong, some even large enough to house the enormity of Mammat. The only entrance into the city via land was on the southern wall where a huge, metal gate was sealed shut. Beyond the gate, two colossal watchtowers were manned by several Human watchers wearing red. Atop both towers was a scarlet flag flapping angrily in the wind.

To the north of the city was the ocean, where the skies were darker than Garrin had ever seen before, and lightning flashed viciously within the clouds. No walls guarded Fervia from the waves that crashed onto its sandy black shores, but neither did they need to. No rebellion force could mount an attack from the water because no force in Pharia had ships, and Jowra obviously didn't consider such defences a priority.

Aquila hovered above the trees while Kivali and Onca broke out of the forest and cantered towards the wall of the city. Garrin watched them dodge the guards and teleport inside, then he patted Aquila fondly on the neck.

"Let's do this," he said confidently.

Aquila straightened her wings and swooped to where Kivali and Onca were heading. Within moments, the watchers in the towers had spotted their arrival and their trumpeting horns combined with the growling thunder.

Garrin focused his mind, and as he and Aquila soared above Kivali and Onca's charge, he forged a powerful tornado of dark sand and stone that led them through the city. The tornado was small at first, barely powerful enough to rattle old hinges. But within seconds, anything loose in the streets was lifted into a mighty vortex, and any wooden doors were ripped from their frames.

"Keep flying," Garrin urged Aquila. *"The more destruction we cause, the more time we buy Torvanon."*

Garrin was sure the roar of the cyclone had attracted the attention of every soldier in Fervia already. But only when they had flown to the far side of the city did Aquila land and Garrin dismount. They were in an open space beyond Fervia's stone buildings, the perfect spot from which to assess the damage they had caused. The stone buildings were still standing, but a trail of broken wood lay in their wake.

"That will have done the trick," Kivali said as she and Onca stopped beside them. She brushed her dark hair out of her face.

Garrin's mind was drawn away from his power and the tornado dwindled to nothing. "I'd be surprised if a single soldier is still guarding the gate," he said confidently.

As if his words were a cue, a rumble of many footsteps met his ears and an army in red marched out of the dust that was yet to settle. The army was close to three-thousand strong, made up mostly of Humans and Grevlors with swords and shields. But here and there, a Lisor stood tall and broad, dragging a heavy wooden club along the sand behind it.

Garrin was jubilant for a moment, but then realised he faced an entire legion with only one other Rider and two Lavorians. Even with their powers, it seemed like an impossible task.

"Ten-thousand wouldn't defeat us," an ever-optimistic Aquila said with assurance.

The enemy force moved forwards in unison. Those nearest seemed brutish and cruel, and those furthest away were faceless but carrying bows.

"Why are they all wearing armour?" Kivali questioned anxiously. "Were they expecting our arrival?"

"I don't know, but I hope Torvanon hurries up!"

Kivali lifted her bow from her back and fired an arrow towards the horde that confronted them. A single, unfortunate Grevlor in the front line took the arrow to the throat. For a moment there was shocked silence, then a cry of fury rose from the vast enemy ranks. Almost immediately, hundreds of arrows were returned from the rearmost fighters, and an arced wave of metal sailed towards them.

"That was a terrible idea!" Garrin yelled at Kivali as he rushed to hide behind Aquila.

The arrows thudded the ground around them and clanged against Aquila and Onca's armour. When all the arrows had landed, Garrin stepped out from behind his Eagle and summoned his tornado once again. When it was of a considerable size, he let it rip through the army, and many who didn't brace themselves fell to the ground or into their comrades. Kivali took advantage of the hysteria and fired several more arrows from her bow, but when the ground began to tremble, Garrin's power failed him and Kivali was forced to step back.

"He's here!" Garrin shouted worriedly.

The enemy ranks parted and allowed a huge creature to break through the clouds of dust. It was Mammat, the Elephant Lavorian larger than any other beast Garrin had seen in his life. His silver armour was dull in the rain, but his long trunk and huge tusks were shimmering with rainwater. Upon his back, barely visible from the ground, Zarad stood with a smirk on his face. His olive skin was painted with white patterns as it had been in Alvoria, and his damp hair flowed down his back.

"Ah, the Rider from Afarra has a pretty girl with him," the Rider mocked. His voice was loud and clear, despite being so high up. "Perhaps he'll feel brave enough in her presence to stand and fight me this time."

Garrin didn't respond; he couldn't respond. He wished his silence was born of arrogance and a need to stall Zarad, but it was merely because he was so terrified of Mammat.

"Have you lost your tongue?" Zarad provoked. "You dare attack King Jowra's city, yet you lack the courage to answer my questions!"

"I'm not scared of you!" Garrin finally replied, but his words were not the truth.

"He speaks!" Zarad yelled to the fighters standing beneath him. They bellowed in reply, mocking Garrin. "Why are you here, Riders of Afarra?"

"To kill every foul creature in this city that fights for Jowra!" Kivali shouted. "Including you."

Zarad laughed. "Just the two of you and your Lavorians?" he asked.

"We don't need more than two Riders to destroy this

place," Garrin said, finding courage from somewhere.

"So the legion of men marching from the forest towards our southern gate are a figment of my imagination, are they?" Zarad said, raising his eyebrows knowingly. "We aren't foolish, you know. We foresaw your plot several days ago."

Garrin bit his lip. "Yet still you've marched thousands of soldiers to meet the four of us. You have no men defending your gate now."

"Actually, Gravaz and Lapsin have led most of our forces to the gate." Zarad laughed again. "After the fiasco in Alvoria, which I admit was my fault, the King didn't consider it wise to risk another city. We have more than enough soldiers to defeat your whole army. Not a single man of yours will step foot inside Fervia's walls."

An almighty crash came from the south of the city and Zarad snapped his head around. He cursed loudly, then seemed to get caught in two minds; whether to fight Garrin and Kivali, or rush to Fervia's gate. In the distance, a plume of dust rose from between the two handsome watchtowers.

"Take my hand," Kivali ordered Garrin.

When he reached out, she grabbed him tightly and held Aquila and Onca too. Suddenly, the world began to spin, and the sight of Zarad and Mammat was lost to darkness.

When he felt his feet touch the ground again, Garrin momentarily gathered himself. They had teleported away from danger and were now stood outside the southern entrance of Fervia, with friendly soldiers bolting past them. The formidable metal gate now lay crumpled on the black sand, and thousands of men were scrambling into the city. It seemed Torvanon had ripped the gate free of the wall, leaving a huge gap through which his army could infiltrate. There, the noise of wind and thunder were nothing compared to the triumphant bellow of Torvanon's soldiers.

"Let's get up high," Garrin said to Aquila. He jumped onto his Eagle's back again, and they rose as Kivali and Onca ran to join Torvanon and Ursus ahead of them. Soldiers were entering the city now, and from the sky, they looked much like ants entering an anthill. They dispersed in every direction, navigating narrow paths between the stone buildings until they came to an area of yellow grass that was vast and smooth.

When Aquila descended and found the roof of a building to perch on, Garrin was able to focus on the field ahead of him. A field guarded by a force on the far side even larger than what had marched out the dust before with Zarad and Mammat.

Garrin grimaced at the immensity of the army, and that was before he noticed Gravaz at the front. The muscular Ulatori was straddling Lapsin, a Hyena Lavorian with a wicked face and foam bubbling at the corners of his mouth. Together, they prowled back and forth, eyeing the men who dared confront them in their own territory.

Torvanon and Ursus were soon to reach the field with their men. Torvanon was resplendent in his gold armour, while Ursus seemed imperiously large, dwarfing even Lapsin opposite him. They were soon followed by Kivali and Onca, and then Horvos joined them on foot too.

"Ready your arrows, comrades," Torvanon commanded.

As bows were pulled off backs and arrows drawn, Garrin watched Zarad and Mammat appear at the back of the enemy force. Another three-thousand men would be following him too.

"Aim. Fire!"

A wave of arrows arced through the sky. In flight, Garrin wondered how many would bring down a foe. He hoped all eight-thousand would drop, but it would have taken a miracle. Had he scouted Fervia and seen a force this large, he wouldn't have advised Torvanon to attack.

The arrows fell like the rain, but Jowra's army quickly moved as one, crouching beneath round shields that would protect them. When barely a body tumbled, Garrin felt a pang of dread.

"We are outnumbered almost three to one, Torvanon!" he shouted. Aquila pushed off from the building and swooped down to Ursus's side.

"Yes, they seem to have gathered quite an army," Torvanon responded. He offered Garrin a smile.

"Do you find it funny?" Garrin said incredulously.

"Of course! This may be the day I die. Why lose your life in misery when you can lose it in euphoria?"

Garrin shook his head. *"No matter which side is victorious, a lot of lives will be lost today,"* he said to Aquila.

As Garrin focused again on the enemy, he heard Ursus sniffing the air beside him.

"There is a strange scent upon the wind," the Bear uttered in his deep timbre. "This weather is driven by something."

"And the air is unusually cold," Horvos added, his gruff voice raised so he could be heard over the building storm.

Onca breathed in too, and then Kivali looked around worriedly.

"They're anxious," Aquila said in Garrin's mind. *"Something has caught their attention."*

"What can you smell?" Garrin asked aloud.

"Whatever it is, it isn't Human," Onca replied.

Garrin pointed across the battlefield. "There are Grevlors and Lisors over there. Could it be them?"

"No. It's a scent I haven't encountered before," Ursus growled. "It isn't of this land."

"Then which land is it from?" Garrin asked, suddenly disturbed by Ursus's revelation.

But the answer did not come, for Jowra's soldiers had begun to beat their shields with the hilts of their weapons. The noise was scattered at first, but it soon became a loud, repetitive drum that made the hairs on the back of Garrin's neck stand.

"Find your courage, men!" Torvanon shouted to the legion behind him.

The noise of the enemy grew ever more, but the Afarran army stood ready, braced for the battle they knew they must win.

"Draw your weapons!" Torvanon ordered. He lifted his sword above his head and the soldiers roared.

"Attack!"

As one, the men charged through the rain at the forbidding force that opposed them. Ursus and Onca carried Torvanon and Kivali across the battlefield faster than the soldiers, and Garrin took to the sky with Aquila. He held his bow in his hand, ready to fire arrows into the enemy ranks, but he struggled to hold steady in the storm.

The response of the enemy to Afarra's approach was to fire a cloud of steel from their own bows. The arrows zigzagged through the air because of the wind, but they were on target. Aquila was forced to roll her body to avoid the attack, but the soldiers below weren't to be so lucky. Yet, before the arrows could land, they all stopped mid-flight. Garrin spotted Torvanon with his hand outstretched, his mind focused on his power even while Ursus bounded across the ground beneath him. He held the arrows steady for a moment, then as the two armies were to collide, he made a throwing gesture with his fist and the arrows thudded into Jowra's front line, killing many.

When the men came together, the clash of weapons and shields was almost lost in the howling wind. Another rumble of thunder came, this time much closer to Fervia, and Garrin watched the black clouds churning and flashing purple above the ocean. The gales were now so strong that Garrin was having to clench Aquila tighter with his legs not to fall.

"We have to land," he said. *"I can barely see the ground through the rain now. I won't know if my arrows are striking friend or foe."*

Hundreds of bodies had already fallen when Aquila landed and Garrin alighted. But the sight of a Rider and Lavorian attracted many enemy fighters who were very much alive: the prize for killing a Rider was to inherit his power *and* Lavorian. But killing a Rider was much harder to do than it seemed. Before Garrin's feet had even hit the grass, he had drawn his sword and killed a Grevlor. A minute later, and a dozen more Grevlors and Humans had been cut down, and his power had disabled a Lisor too.

The fighting intensified as more bodies fell and the ferocious storm drew ever nearer. Bolts of lightning now lit up the battlefield, and the rumbles of thunder that ultimately followed drowned out the screams of the fighters who Garrin and Aquila stabbed with sword and beak. The cold rain turned to sleet and Garrin found himself being dragged towards the centre of the battle where the other Riders were fighting. He ducked and dodged the attacks of adversaries and continued to slay anyone who stood in his way. The Grevlors and Humans were easy to kill, so long as he found the gaps in their armour. The Lisors, however, were trickier. It took a powerful thrust to force a blade through their thick skin, and it then took several seconds to pull it free. Every time a Lisor fell, Garrin relied on Aquila to protect him while he retrieved his sword.

Soon, Garrin was beside Horvos, with Torvanon and Kivali somewhere nearby. Between them, they slaughtered many, but Garrin expected the battle to change when they were met by Gravaz or Zarad. Through the storm, it was impossible to see more than a few yards ahead now, and aside from a few flashes of exploding fire every so often, Garrin had no idea where either Rider was. Even more worryingly, he couldn't see Lapsin or Mammat, despite their considerable size.

"This is madness, Torvanon!" Garrin heard Horvos bellow over the sound of the storm. "We need to fall back."

"No, keep fighting! We cannot retreat because of the weather," came Torvanon's response.

Horvos wiped the rain from his face and grimaced. But he obediently fought on, swinging his axe like it weighed no more than a letter-opener.

"You should take to the sky and find Gravaz or Zarad," Garrin said to Aquila. He stabbed a man through the heart, then watched Kivali teleport and remove a Grevlor's head from its shoulders.

"Will you be okay by yourself?" Aquila asked.

Garrin summoned his power and blasted the falling rain in every direction. The force of the strike knocked more than twenty fighters onto their backs. *"I'm sure I'll be fine,"* he said.

Aquila took off and Garrin finished off several of the Grevlors he'd taken down. Then he backed off from a furious Lisor before driving his blade into its bellowing mouth.

For a while, Garrin did nothing but kill enemies. But when his arms started to ache, he wondered how many more fighters would oppose him. There were eight-thousand enemy fighters, and they came out the storm in endless droves. A significant number of them were dead around him already, but so too were the soldiers of Afarra. The battle was a massacre, and it was nothing more than lives being traded. In the end, the victor would be the army with Riders still standing.

"Aquila, we must defeat Gravaz and Zarad if we're to bring this battle to an end," Garrin voiced in his mind.

Aquila didn't respond. There were just screams of men and the rumbling sky.

"Aquila, are you there?"

"You're in luck, Rider," she finally answered. *"Look up!"*

Garrin pulled his blade free of a Grevlors ribs and then squinted up through the rain. Above him, Aquila swooped acrobatically out the storm clouds, followed closely by an Elephant's trunk. The Elephant's tusks came next, then a colossal head with wild, narrow eyes. The ground quaked violently as Mammat stepped into view of the Riders of Afarra, and the fighting came to a sudden halt. Every Human, Grevlor and Lisor lowered its weapon and faced the Elephant Lavorian and its brave challengers.

"How are we going to kill that monster?" Horvos barked through the wind. He gripped the handle of his axe tightly with damp hands and anxiously gazed upwards.

"With a lot of good fortune," Torvanon said in return. The leader's gold armour was wet with rain and blood, and he looked exhausted. He was no longer riding Ursus, but the Bear stood dutifully at his side. Compared to Mammat, Ursus looked like a regular-sized Lavorian. He wasn't even half the Elephant's size.

Aquila landed next to Garrin and squawked loudly. Garrin stroked her neck, and then her call was answered by Mammat, whose trunk bellowed so loudly it shook the clouds.

"You did well," Garrin said, covering his ears with his hands. *"But how are we going to bring him down?"*

On top of Mammat's head, Garrin could see Zarad waving his fist threateningly. Because of the wind, he couldn't hear the words the Rider was shouting, but he was sure they would be something derogatory. The white paint had washed off his face now, but the evil grin still remained.

The soldiers surrounding the Riders and Lavorians had formed a crowd when Garrin looked. The fighting between them seemed to have ceased, and they stood together in red, green and blue. It was unusual to see, as was four Riders and Lavorians within striking distance of each other.

"Stand together," Kivali urged. "The three of us can defeat him now he's alone."

"The four of us!" Horvos corrected. "Don't forget about me."

But that's when Lapsin prowled from the storm with Gravaz upon his back. They stood alongside Mammat and Zarad, comparatively small, but intimidating nonetheless. Now that Mammat wasn't alone, Garrin's chest tightened in fear.

"Use the rain to extinguish his fire, Garrin," Torvanon demanded loudly. "I can defend us from any weapons except fire." He patted Ursus's foreleg and had a quiet moment with the Bear. "Kivali, if you get the opportunity to teleport and kill one of the Riders, take it. Onca and Aquila, the same applies to you."

"What about me?" Horvos shouted. "What's my task?"

"Keep your distance," Torvanon ordered. "This isn't a fight for you."

"Are you mad?" Horvos bellowed. He swung his axe fiercely through the air. "I'm made for battles like these!"

But the moment he finished, Gravaz summoned a fireball and launched it in Horvos's direction. The explosion came at his feet and threw him backwards onto the wet ground. A second fireball came, but Garrin quenched it with a jet of water before it could cause any more damage. The crowd groaned like they were watching a theatre performance in Torvanon's palace.

In response to the attack on his friend, Torvanon raised his hand and lifted all the abandoned arrows and swords from the ground. With a thrust of his fist, the weapons were thrown at Gravaz, but the Ulatori rolled from Lapsin's back and used the Hyena as his shield. The clang against the Lavorian's armour sounded distant within the roar of the storm, and Gravaz's angry cursing was lost altogether.

With the enemy distracted, Ursus and Onca charged forwards, while Aquila shot into the sky and Kivali vanished from sight. As Ursus and Onca approached Lapsin, Mammat's huge trunk swung through the air and flung the two Lavorians aside as if they weighed no more than a starved Grevlor each. The attack left Garrin,

Torvanon and Horvos exposed, and Gravaz aimed another fireball at them. Garrin reduced it to ash once again, then sent a powerful jet of rainwater back at the Ulatori and almost knocked him off his feet.

"Are Ursus and Onca okay, Aquila?" Garrin asked worriedly.

"Ursus is okay, but Onca is still down. Kivali is going to her now."

"Do they need help?"

"I'll go to them while you keep fighting," Aquila replied, swooping over the battlefield. *"Be careful though, Zarad is dismounting."*

Sure enough, Zarad was sliding down Mammat's trunk when Garrin looked up. When he landed beside Gravaz, he seemed to delight in the chaos. His face was as sadistically excited as Garrin had expected it to be.

"Do you mind if I join the fun?" he shouted happily. His face contorted into an evil smile.

The three men who faced him merely stared. They were impressed with his elegant dismount, but equally ready to chop off his head.

"Does anybody from Afarra speak?" he mocked as he placed his hands on his hips.

"I'll cut your restless tongue out your mouth!" Horvos threatened, losing patience. He lifted his axe and sprinted towards Zarad.

"Horvos, stop!" Torvanon demanded.

But Horvos ignored his leader's order and continued forwards. Garrin's heart skipped a beat as he saw Zarad's hand rise, and he too shouted for Horvos to halt. But it was in vain. Torvanon used his power to throw Horvos aside, but Zarad had been quicker. And when Horvos hit the ground, he had several red-feathered darts stuck in his face and neck. Time seemed to slow down as helplessness and sorrow flooded Garrin's body. He heard Horvos's groan of pain and Torvanon's bellow of despair, then he heard Zarad's laughter. Before he knew what he was doing, Garrin was charging at Zarad himself with his sword held out in front of him. He was going to make him regret his actions.

"Garrin, no! He'll do to you what he did to Horvos!"

But before Garrin could slaughter the man who had killed his friend, Zarad was thrown high into the air with Gravaz and Lapsin by what could only be Torvanon's power. Garrin stopped and turned around to see his leader stood still beneath the storm clouds, a look of fury in his usually warm eyes. He was pointing a single finger beyond Garrin at the giant Elephant Lavorian, and despite his ginger beard flapping in the wind, his concentration was unwavering. Garrin turned back to see Mammat's black eyes narrowed in fear, and his trunk swinging wildly from side to side. The crowd of soldiers that had gathered gaped in silence as the enormous Lavorian rose slowly off the ground, and they all covered their ears as he trumpeted his objections. Up and up he went until his four feet were higher than Ursus, and then Torvanon dropped him back to the ground. Mammat's legs buckled under his weight and he fell onto his side, while the ground shook and threw every soldier onto his back. The only man left standing was Torvanon.

"That was incredible!" Aquila voiced inside Garrin's head.

Garrin momentarily forgot about Zarad's attack on Horvos and nodded his head. *"His power is stronger than I thought possible."*

"We need to kill their Riders while Mammat is down!" Aquila said. She glided through the sky towards Garrin, but a bolt of lightning flashed down from the clouds and knocked her out the sky.

"Aquila!"

The Eagle hit the ground hard and churned up the sodden turf. Garrin made to run over to her, but several more bolts came down, deafening and bright, and kept them separated.

"I'm okay," Aquila assured him. *"I'll come to you."*

The storm clouds surged and the winds built to a gale. The battlefield suddenly became very dark and was lit only by the flashes of lightning that crackled overhead. Thoughts of war became the least of Garrin's worries as he waited in fear for Aquila to come and save him.

"We must leave now or we'll die here!" Ursus warned as he ran to where Garrin and Torvanon were standing. "The Fizorachis are coming!"

From the north of the battlefield, Garrin spotted an incoming force of creatures in black armour that, together, looked like a wave of oil washing over soldiers both dead and alive. Initially, he felt relief as Jowra's soldiers were the first to fall victim to this new force, but then he began to panic when he realised he and his comrades would be next to die.

"A Rider's powers are depleted when Fizorachis are near," Ursus boomed. "You can't fight them off so get out of here before they kill you!"

Garrin was quick to project his thoughts onto his Lavorian. *"You heard him. We need to go!"*

"I'm on my way. Stay where you are."

The incoming Fizorachis caused chaos across the

battlefield. As the other soldiers saw what was coming, they all turned to the southern gate and tripped over each other in their attempt to escape.

As Aquila swooped and dodged between the numerous strikes of lightning, Garrin watched Torvanon approach Horvos and kneel.

"Why are you still here?" Horvos wheezed from the floor. "You should be fleeing."

Torvanon lifted his friend's head with one hand and pulled Zarad's darts out of his face with the other. Despite the panic around him, he seemed very calm. "I would regret not saying goodbye." A tear fell from his eye and trickled into his beard. "I would take you with me, but I can no longer carry you. They've drained me of my power."

"I understand," Horvos said. "Just promise me one thing."

"Go on," Torvanon prompted.

"Promise me you'll win the war."

Torvanon smiled ruefully. "When the war is over, people will sing songs of your courage today."

Horvos coughed and Garrin saw blood spray onto his chin. His life was coming to its end whether the Fizorachis reached him or not.

Torvanon lowered Horvos's head and stood. He turned to Garrin. "Go back to Afarra and warn the people of what's happening here. It will be quicker for you and Aquila by flight."

"But what about you and Kivali?" Garrin asked.

Torvanon mounted Ursus and Kivali and Onca arrived at his side. "We'll outrun the Fizorachis on our Lavorians. Don't worry about us."

Garrin nodded his head at Torvanon and stepped into the path of Aquila's flight. He raised his arms and she snatched him with her claws and lifted him towards the clouds above. Lightning crackled around them, but Garrin felt safer as soon as he was above the ground.

Below, Torvanon and Kivali were already riding Ursus and Onca towards Fervia's destroyed gate. Alongside them, Mammat was fleeing too with Zarad back on his head. The Elephant had got back to his feet again after Torvanon's attack and was shaking the ground with every thundering footstep. Behind them, the Fizorachis glided over the land, turning the ground black and butchering everything in their path. The soldiers fell in their thousands, barely able to put up a fight.

"Aquila, stop!" Garrin demanded.

She slowed to a hover. *"What's wrong?"*

"Look at Gravaz and Lapsin," he said. *"They've stopped."*

The Rider and Lavorian had indeed come to a halt, and Gravaz held out his hand in a gesture for the Fizorachis to slaughter no more. When they reached him, the entire army came to a stop, and Garrin was able to get a better look at them. In their thousands they stood, all tall and pale, and stood like Humans on two legs. They wore black armour that glistened in the rain, and wielded light swords that were perfect for killing with the speed in which they moved. They were a terrifying race to look at, with hollows in their faces seeming to carry the darkness of the storm that followed them.

Garrin was surprised the Fizorachis stopped for Gravaz. He had expected them to slice through him just like they had everyone else, but they appeared to sense his power. Either that or they cared not for killing the Lavorian beside him. Lapsin was stood wilder than ever, his eyes darting from left to right and froth dripping from his mouth. He looked concerned, and for good reason. With Gravaz powerless, he was the only protection his Rider had from instant death.

For a second, not much happened. The race in black stared at Gravaz, and the Ulatori stared back. The storm continued to encircle them, and the rain came down like it was pouring from a hose. But then a large beast advanced from within the ranks of the Fizorachis, and Garrin let out a gasp. The beast wasn't totally unlike a Lavorian, although the animal it resembled Garrin did not recognise. It was the size of Ursus and covered in sharp spines from its thick head down to its four short legs. It had a long, thin tail and three red eyes that moved independently of each other, one in the centre of its face and the other two on either side of its head. It had a large mouth full of several rows of teeth, and its armour, instead of silver like a Lavorian's, was jet black like the army around it. Riding upon the beast was a Fizorachi far more impressive than those beneath him. He was taller and broader than his comrades, with more majestic armour and a large two-ended sword. He was certainly the leader of the army, and as he was carried towards Gravaz by his beast, the Fizorachis around him screeched in delight.

When the Fizorachi leader dismounted, Garrin realised how immense he truly was. He dwarfed Gravaz in size, just as his beast dwarfed Lapsin, and Garrin was glad it was the Ulatori being confronted and not himself.

With each step the Fizorachi took towards Gravaz, the sky flashed with lightning and the grass at his feet withered. Despite his hatred for the Ulatori, Garrin respected his courage for not fleeing like everyone else. But with that respect came uncertainty, and Garrin wondered why Gravaz was willing to risk his life to face the Fizorachis alone. Then the two began to converse, and Garrin's uncertainty grew ever more. It became clear that Gravaz didn't wish to fight the invaders, he was welcoming them instead.

"They're negotiating," he said worriedly to Aquila. *"He's trying to convince them to unite with Jowra's forces."*

But as the unpleasant feeling was building in Garrin's stomach, he sensed a sudden change in the Fizorachi's mood. The storm built to its most ferocious yet and Garrin struggled to stay on Aquila's back. Rods of lightning struck the ground and left craters all around, while the rain became hail. The Fizorachis screamed euphorically, and their leader raised a hand to Gravaz's chest. When the explosion of purple light erupted from his palm, the Ulatori was thrown through the air and onto his back. Lapsin snarled and leapt at his Rider's attacker in retaliation, but the Fizorachi was too fast. With speed and precision, he brought down the blade of his sword and sliced the Lavorian's head from its body.

Garrin put his hands on his head and swore. *"What! I didn't think Lavorians could be killed by swords!"* he cried out.

The storm seemed to ease at Lapsin's death. The clouds didn't swirl so much, and the cold hail reduced to light, warm rain. But Gravaz's roar of despair was enough to make Garrin shiver more than he had all day. Some of the Fizorachi soldiers moved forwards to restrain the Ulatori and drag him away from his Lavorian, while their leader mounted his beast again and rode away without a second glance.

Stunned and distressed, Garrin rubbed the back of Aquila's neck. *"Let's get out of here,"* he uttered.

Aquila was quick to oblige and beat her wings to gain some height. Veering west, she made for the sky above the Raspian Forest that looked safe and blue.

From behind them, a beautiful silver orb appeared from inside Lapsin's headless body and rose peacefully into the sky. It lingered briefly above the army of Fizorachis, then vanished and allowed the storm to rage once more.

A Lavorian had been killed, and the battle of Fervia was over.

EIGHTEEN

Joura's Powers

Having escaped Malum, Oracus and Bandor made camp in the boscage on the far side of the river. They were loathed to stop so close to the city, but they had little choice of shelter other than that one area of trees. Thankfully, Xintora and Jhaqar didn't pursue them, and they were able to recover some sleep.

After months of living in snow, Oracus was glad to finally feel warmth on his skin. They were only a hundred metres beyond the river, but the temperature was much higher than that of the icy land they had left behind. In fact, he could see the snow still falling there if he squinted through the trees. Oracus remembered Kivali and Quent explaining this phenomenon to him when he was still in Afarra. The Great River separates the freezing lands in the south from the hotter lands in the north – one bank is laden with snow, the other with white sand.

As daylight seeped through the leaves of the trees, Oracus and Bandor progressed onto the scorching desert beyond, where heat-haze flooded the terrain for miles into the distance. Oracus wasn't sure whether it was because the desert was exceptionally hot, or because he had adapted to the climate in Valaroth, but he soon had sweat dripping off his face, and he wished he'd taken more water from the river.

They travelled for hours and the sun got ever hotter. By mid-afternoon, Oracus was exhausted and sore. The sun had burnt his neck and face, and Bandor's leather saddle was too hot to sit on, so he was forced to walk.

"What's the point of being a Rider if I can't actually ride?" he grumbled unhappily.

Bandor sniggered. *"We've travelled to huge cities and survived deadly encounters with other Riders, but now you're complaining about a bit of sand in your boots?"*

"Don't make me feel worse," Oracus replied, frowning. *"I just want to find some water and have a sit down."*

"There's water over there," Bandor said nonchalantly.

Oracus looked up hopefully and scanned the horizon, but saw only heat-haze.

"It looks like a lake to me, we're heading straight for it," Bandor added.

"I can't see anything," Oracus said. *"Are you sure?"*

Bandor rolled his eyes. *"Yes, I'm sure."*

"Wait, how long have you known there's a lake over there?"

"I don't know. A couple of hours maybe."

"And you didn't think to tell me?" Oracus growled unhappily.

"You're my Rider. You should know what I'm thinking," Bandor said with a shrug.

Oracus opened his mouth but couldn't find the words to protest. He decided his efforts would be better spent reaching the lake than moaning at Bandor. *"Come on then, what are you waiting for?"* he said. Then he started to run.

In no time, they arrived at their destination. What Oracus

had expected to be a small pool of water turned out to be a vast lake, just as Bandor had said. The water was blue and clear, with a shimmer of sunlight reflecting in its surface and fish basking in the warm shallows. There were palm trees growing all around the lake's edge, with birds singing merrily in the branches.

Exhausted and thirsty, Oracus threw off his armour and dived headlong into the water. It was cool and refreshing, and as he submerged, he realised how much he'd missed living in the north.

"Aren't you going to join me?" he asked Bandor as he came back to the surface.

Oracus could sense the Lion's reservation as he eyed the water suspiciously. *"I've only been in water once before and that was when Gravaz dumped us in the ocean after fighting him in Tallarin. I don't have fond memories of it."*

"Oh, come on. This is hardly like that. The ocean was deep and freezing; this is quite pleasant."

Reluctantly, Bandor dipped a paw into the water and screwed up his face in displeasure. But as he edged closer to Oracus, he became more confident and started splashing.

"See, it's not so bad," Oracus said.

Bandor pranced around happily for a few seconds, but then stumbled as he reached the deeper water and fell under. He came back up spluttering, and quickly paddled back to the bank where he would be safe.

Oracus howled with laughter while Bandor shook the water from his metal fur.

"Never again!" the Lion exclaimed. And he lay down on the sand to dry off.

They enjoyed the lake for a while (Oracus more so than

Bandor after his accident) and made the most of a chance to have fun – something that had been very hard to come by during recent months. When they eventually moved on, they rounded the lake to the west, with Oracus feeling reinvigorated. They passed a small herd of wildebeest using the water as a drinking-hole, and watched birds swooping over the lake to feast on fry swimming in shoals on the surface.

But as they reached the western bank of the lake, Oracus was consumed by a feeling of anger that blocked his senses. His sight flickered and the smell of the lake left him too. Then the songs of the birds were lost to the whirring in his ears. He suddenly felt a presence in his mind of such immense power that it threatened to cripple him.

"Oracus, what's wrong?" Bandor's voice was barely a whisper beyond the pain.

Oracus tried to control his thoughts and open his eyes, but all he saw were dark walls and heavy snow. He blinked furiously, confused, and looked up to see not a blue sky, but a snowy sky with Wravias and Pseubas gliding through it.

Oracus shook his head and managed to focus on Bandor for a few seconds. *"It's Jowra. I can feel his mind. I'm in his head,"* he grunted.

With difficulty, Bandor entered his mind and eased the pressure, taking half the burden himself. It was a relief, like he had been granted air after a minute without. He opened his eyes again and saw sunlight, sand and water. And now he was stable, he realised his vision had been of the keep in Melzor.

"Thank you," Oracus uttered. *"I think he's found out we escaped Malum."*

Oracus could tell by how acute the pain was that Jowra was nearby, but he didn't expect to see a city in the distance when he looked. Through the heat-haze, it was difficult to make out, but two tiny black specks could be seen gliding high above it.

"That's Melzor!" Oracus exclaimed. *"And those dots are Wravias and Pseubas!"*

Bandor searched the horizon until he found the city. Then his eyes opened wide. Feeling a combination of Bandor's fear and Jowra's fury was an unusual experience for Oracus, and he wished it would disappear.

"I didn't realise we were so close," Bandor said.

The anger spiked again and Oracus tried to push the feeling aside. But he was back in the keep, with a blizzard beginning to build around him. Snowflakes struck his face and made him feel good, and the screeches of his Dragons were divine. Strangely, Oracus could hear the Dragons' shrieks through both Jowra's ears and his own.

"We need to get away from here," Oracus cried. *"We have nowhere to hide if he realises where we are."*

Oracus jumped into Bandor's saddle and disregarded the pain of it burning his legs. But the Lavorian didn't move.

"Bandor, we need to go!" Oracus urged.

"Not yet. If you're close enough to feel his mind then you're close enough to learn his powers," Bandor said, somehow pushing aside his fear to think with clarity. *"We can't pass up an opportunity like this."*

Oracus considered Bandor's suggestion and ran his hands through the Lion's mane. It felt good to have a Lavorian so intelligent, and no longer did he feel so rushed to leave.

"But what if he can feel me using his powers? I don't want to

alert him to our presence."

"No other Riders can feel it. Why would he?"

"Because he's King Jowra," Oracus said worriedly. *"The most powerful Rider who ever lived."*

"If that happens, I'll get us to the Raspian Forest before he can catch us."

Oracus looked at Bandor and trusted him completely. He nodded, and then began to fight Jowra's might so he could focus on his powers instead.

At first, none presented themselves. Oracus felt like he'd popped the lid on a barrel but found nothing inside. But then a flutter of excitement came to him as he linked with several powers he'd never experienced before.

"He has so many!" Oracus declared. As he spoke, he felt his limbs become lighter and he started to rise off Bandor's back. He floated for a second, trying to keep his balance, and then fell onto the sand as his focus lapsed. *"He can fly!"*

Bandor walked impatiently around Oracus, eager for more. *"What else can he do?"*

With new-found vigour, Oracus began embracing the strength of Jowra's mind instead of trying to escape it. It was tough, but with Bandor's help, he could ignore the anger and channel the powers. Soon, it became difficult to use only one at a time.

"He can summon lightning," Oracus said. He felt a surge run down his arms and saw purple light crackling at his fingertips. It was warm and tingled his hands pleasantly.

The next power came as a shock. Before Oracus had finished trying to control the lightning, a scolding heat ran down his leg. He grabbed the handle of his sword and pulled it out its sheath to reveal a blade rippling with orange flames. *"He can bring fire to his weapons too!"* he cried fervently.

The fire extinguished and Oracus's excitement built ever more as he returned his sword to his belt. Discovering the array of Jowra's powers had at first been frightening, but now he couldn't have been more determined to overthrow him.

"Let me feel the full force of his mind again, Bandor," he said hungrily.

Bandor adhered to his request and Oracus groaned as the pressure in his mind built. It took a lot of control, but he was now able to withstand Jowra's mind, and it was more wonderful than he would ever have imagined. He floated upwards again, with his hands outstretched and his cloak billowing around him. The walls of the keep no longer confined him, and he was at the mercy of the sky; the sky that he controlled. When he reached the heights of Wravias and Pseubas, he hung in the air, studying them both with red eyes. The blizzard around them began to build until the storm was so dense it was like being trapped in ice. The snow became hail and the clouds began to rumble with thunder, yet still the storm grew more intense.

It was only when Wravias and Pseubas screamed that the blizzard eased. The Dragons had been battling to remain airborne, but Jowra hadn't cared. His rage had been so profound that he'd have let them fall to their deaths.

It was then that Oracus was brought back into his own body. Bandor was in his mind again, urging him to calm down, but the anger had been all-consuming this time. He hadn't even realised that he'd entered Jowra's mind.

"Don't let me do that again," Oracus said, suddenly fearful. *"That was too much."*

"Are you okay?" Bandor asked him.

"I think so."

"He can control the weather too, can't he?" Bandor said.

Oracus looked to the west and saw the storm he'd just been at the centre of. It had been so cold and terrifying. *"He can do so much more too,"* he mumbled with a shake of his head. *"His mind is beyond anything I can comprehend. I can't withstand it alone. It's like a thousand Riders' minds rolled into one."*

Bandor eyed him anxiously and waited for him to stand before speaking. *"What are his other powers?"*

"I don't know," Oracus said. *"I could sense them, but I couldn't grasp them well enough to use them."*

"Do you think those were powers that required specific conditions to work?" Bandor suggested. *"Like we know he can revive Riders, because that's what he did to your mother. But you wouldn't be able to copy it without a dead Rider here to use it on."*

"That's a good theory, and I think you're probably right," Oracus agreed. But the mention of his mother was a shock that knocked him sideways. He had gone so long without thinking of her that suddenly he felt very emotional. A tear trickled down his cheek as he remembered firing the arrow through her heart.

"I'm sorry, Oracus. I didn't mean to upset you," Bandor said sadly.

Oracus waved his hand dismissively and climbed onto his Lavorian's back. *"We should get moving,"* he said.

Bandor was quick to oblige and started trotting over the sand. To their left, the storm had faded and the Dragons were no longer flying over their King's city.

"The forest can't be too far away now," Bandor said reassuringly. *"I can smell the trees already."*

NINETEEN

The Emerald Pairing

The vast southern border of the Raspian Forest soon crept over the horizon, just as dusk arrived. Barring their break at the lake, Oracus and Bandor had travelled non-stop since leaving the woods at the Great River. Fortuitously, they hadn't encountered a single enemy patrol.

When they finally stepped into the trees, Oracus felt comfort that had been absent for far too long. The forest was the place where he had grown up; hunting game with his bow. It was wonderful to hear birdsong again, and to hear the wind caressing the leaves. In the Black Forest, all that had been missing. An eeriness had resided there, and a silence that wasn't at all natural.

Full night had soon fallen, and the darkness inevitably came. But the darkness wasn't as dense as what Oracus was used to. Through Bandor's eyes, he could still see quite clearly. Hoof prints of deer were evident in the dirt all around, and insects were fluttering between branches. Oracus's other senses were sharp too, he could smell the fungus growing around the tree trunks and hear the scurrying of something small in the undergrowth. He could feel the earthy breeze tickling his face too, and he could feel something else against his leg…

"Bandor, my sword is vibrating!" he shouted out. He held the handle and felt it tremor in his hand.

"Look, the emerald is glowing too," Bandor observed.

Oracus drew the sword from its sheath and examined it. The stone in the hilt was indeed offering a dull green light. *"It's never done this before,"* he said.

"Any idea what it means?" Bandor asked.

Oracus shook his head. He had no idea why it was acting in such a way. He jabbed the sword forwards and then swung it around his body in a figure-of-eight motion, and the vibrations continued. Wondering if it was warning him of something, Oracus turned around, and that's when the vibrations stopped. He stared at the emerald for a second, and watched the light fade away. Then he faced north again and the sword burst back into life.

"I wonder if it's trying to lead us somewhere?" he voiced. He looked at Bandor and saw that the Lion was as intrigued as him. *"Come on, this way!"*

Oracus marched purposefully through the forest with Bandor close behind him. With each step north, the sword became more lively, until it began to tremble violently after several minutes. When the vibrations were so fierce that Oracus could no longer hold the sword, he slid the blade back into its sheath, and that's when they reached a place that made him draw a deep breath.

The emerald was now shining so brightly that Oracus didn't need Bandor's senses to see. He was stood in an abandoned village that appeared to have been destroyed by fire many years ago. The wooden houses were barely houses at all any more. They were as black as the night itself and open to the heavens, with ivy and weeds beginning to devour them.

"There's a sign there," Bandor said. *"I can't quite make out what it says."*

Oracus stepped forwards and wiped away the moss that concealed the words. But he already knew what the words would say.

"Welcome to Emsbleek," Bandor deciphered.

This was the village where Jowra had lived as a child. Oracus had dreamt of it before. It was also the place where his own mother and father had taken refuge after fleeing Melzor.

"I was brought here when I was first born," Oracus said. *"And Jowra's family were killed here too."*

Snippets of dreams flickered in Oracus's memory. He remembered a fourteen-year-old Jowra leading his mother and two younger sisters through the streets of the village to escape a brutal invasion. He had been so innocent then, and so desperate to keep his family safe. Maybe it was his failure as a child that led him to become the tyrannical King of today. Nobody should have to watch their family being dragged away to die, not even Jowra.

Oracus felt pity for his nemesis, and then felt inclined to follow the same path through the village that Jowra and his family had taken when trying to flee. He wandered through the trees and bushes that had grown in the time since, and then stood where the square used to be. That was the exact place where Jowra's life had crumbled from beneath him.

Oracus turned away and retreated to the burnt houses. His sword was now whirring loudly and the emerald blindingly bright. In the near-silence of the forest, it was alarming how conspicuous the sword was being, and Oracus tried to cover its shine with his hand.

Along the route he walked, he spotted a house unlike the others. This one had avoided the fire, yet it had succumbed to nature and was almost invisible behind the ivy. When Oracus decided to approach it, his sword became ever more brazen.

Pulling the ivy aside, Oracus stepped through the door of the house and found himself looking at a room that replicated one of his visions. His mother and father had lived here twenty years ago when he was still a baby, and they had survived with only each other for company. The house was empty, except for a bed and a stove, and the wooden rafters were beginning to surrender to the damp.

An incredible sadness swept over Oracus as he realised that this place was where his family had last been whole. He touched all the surfaces they may once have touched themselves, and hoped to recall a memory that he may since have forgotten. If he listened carefully, he could still hear the faintest echo of their voices and laughter resonating in the walls.

A sudden rattling noise made him jump and drew him from his thoughts. He looked around the room and saw that the metal stove was rocking on its legs and emitting a green light from within. Oracus inched forwards cautiously, and when he opened the stove door, the light faded immediately and his sword stopped vibrating. Now relying on Bandor's senses to see, Oracus reached into the stove and pulled out an emerald necklace and a piece of old parchment. At his touch, the emeralds in both the necklace and sword flashed one last time.

The emerald in the necklace was housed in a spherical

pendant that dangled from a thin, golden chain. It was a necklace Oracus had seen before in his visions – it had been owned by King Xarmoud. The necklace and sword together created a phenomenon called the Emerald Pairing, and it provided a power like no other, but Oracus knew not what it was.

As Oracus's attention switched from the necklace to the parchment, he realised he was holding a note decades old. The words were scrawled untidily, as if the writer had been in a hurry. It read:

I am writing this letter in the hope that one day it will be found and delivered.

I made the most painful choice of my life today, and now I will likely never see my love or our son again. My bones ache with a longing to follow them, but doing so will ensure their death, so I must not.

With all my heart I love them both, and I will think of them always until I pass from this land. I very much hope they read this one day and understand.

I am sorry my time with them ended so abruptly. To Padaquin and Oracus, I will remember you fondly.

Catania.

Oracus dropped the necklace and sword to the floor. It was like time stood still in the abandoned house and he may well have been standing there for a lifetime. He didn't breathe and he didn't see, he just felt despair clutch his heart with a giant fist.

When he finally did breathe, it came in gasps, and that's when the tears came too. Memories of his mother's last moments in Tallarin were quick to resurface. The fury in her face as Jowra controlled her body, the way she ended Alticon's life, and the crimson that flooded her eyes. It was then that Oracus realised he would always remember his mother as the woman who was controlled by the King. Whoever she had been before then was a stranger to him.

An anger built up in Oracus that was all his own, not Jowra's. He yelled out in frustration and kicked the stove hard, desperate to pass his pain on to something else.

Bandor appeared in the doorway of the house and gave Oracus a concerned look. He didn't ask him if he was okay, for that was obvious. He had been in Oracus's mind when he discovered the contents of the stove, so he knew exactly how he felt.

"We'll stay here for the rest of the night," the Lavorian said. *"Try and get some rest and I'll keep guard out here."*

Oracus didn't respond, he just picked up the necklace from the floor and looped it over his head. He lay down on the rotting wooden bed and stared blindly at the ceiling, hoping to remember something uplifting about his mother. But every time he thought of her, those red eyes would stare back at him.

He rolled onto his side after an hour and closed his eyes, hoping that sleep would be his reprieve. He was so tired from the journey north that he was sure he would drift, but his head continued to spin.

He had spent his whole life wanting to meet his mother, and eventually his wish came true. But tonight he was desperate for her to leave him again, even if it was for just a few hours. When she died, he hadn't been given a chance to mourn her, and now finding the letter had brought it all back. Lying there alone, he wept for a while. And when the tears dried up, he tried without success to forget.

Not a moment's sleep was had that night, and not a moment's solace either.

Twenty

Return To Afarra

At some point in the night, Catania's voice had crept into the derelict house, only for Oracus to realise he was imagining it. He had cried again, but only for a short time.

Morning finally arrived and light shone into the room through the broken windows. It was to be a warm day, and the sounds of the forest were that of home. But the homely feel didn't stir Oracus, he remained recumbent on the bed, clutching his mother's note, having read it a thousand times during the night.

"Are you ready to go?" Bandor asked him, poking his head through the door and rustling the ivy.

"No."

"We can't stay here forever, you know."

"I'm not going anywhere."

"Come on, Afarra is less than a day's travel from here."

"Bandor, leave me alone!"

Bandor withdrew and left him a while longer, but was eventually forced to delve into his mind and relieve him of his depression. *"It's time to get up now. I'm putting a stop to this."*

No longer wallowing in self-pity, Oracus gathered himself and rode Bandor out of Emsbleek. Leaving the village may have been heart-breaking had his Lavorian left him with any feelings. But as it was, he left without a care. Although he did still have his mother's note clenched in his fist and the necklace around his neck.

For hours after, they made their way through the forest. The birds in their nests above were full of song and the air was thick with the scent of pines. It was glorious, but for most of it, Oracus felt nothing.

Morning turned to afternoon, then afternoon became evening. And as the tweets of sparrows became the hoots of owls, Oracus and Bandor stepped out the Raspian Forest and were faced with the grassy plains that preceded Afarra. In the distance, the city stood strong and proud in the fading light, and Oracus sighed knowing that Jowra hadn't yet invaded. Bandor allowed Oracus a moment to feel, and his emotion was mostly relief.

"It's still standing," Bandor said happily.

"It's been more than a year since we left Tallarin," Oracus said. *"I thought Jowra would have made his move by now."*

"Let's find out who's still here, shall we?" Bandor suggested.

They reached the drawbridge to Afarra before night had truly fallen, but the orange lamps were being lit by the archers guarding the city from the ramparts. Oracus and Bandor stopped at the edge of the moat where the drawbridge hadn't yet descended.

"State your business here," a voice yelled from up high.

"Oracus and Bandor," Oracus shouted in response. "We're here to see Torvanon."

A bell chimed beyond the wall and then the drawbridge began to lower. That's when Oracus felt the first mind of another Rider from within the city; it was Garrin.

A huge Eagle glided through the air, far bigger than the one left behind over a year ago, and swooped down to the ground beside Oracus and Bandor. Garrin almost fell off Aquila in his excitement to see his friend. "Where have you been?" he said as he pulled him into a firm hug. "We all thought you'd been killed."

Seeing Garrin was the best feeling Oracus had had in a long time, and it temporarily pushed thoughts of his mother away. He held his friend's hug for a while, for it was the first real Human contact he'd felt since Tallarin. "It is so good to see you," he said happily.

Garrin held Oracus at arm's length and looked into his eyes. "You look different," he observed. "Wiser, but worn."

Oracus nodded his head. "It's been quite a journey. But I'm still alive and that's what matters."

"Come on, let's get you inside and fed. You look like you need a good meal." Garrin put an arm around Oracus's shoulder and directed him to the drawbridge.

When they were inside the city, the hustle and bustle was a lot less than it had once been. And when the bell stopped chiming, near silence fell over the streets.

"When I last entered this place, people were falling over each other to meet me," Oracus remembered. "Now it's a lot different."

"The war has taken its toll on Afarra," Garrin replied. "There's less joy these days."

They were heading towards the palace, Oracus realised. He could see its spires in the distance sticking up above the other stone buildings. He wondered if he already had a bed ready for him there.

"Stop!"

A woman's voice was heard behind them and Oracus suddenly felt Dyma's mind in his own. When he turned around, he saw she was with Huadlan and several guards with arrows nocked to their bows. Huadlan was Dyma's Orangutan Lavorian, and he had grown significantly in the last year. When Oracus had still been in Tallarin, the Lavorian could hang from Dyma's shoulders, but now he was taller than her. Dyma herself looked the same as she had before. Her hair was still grey and frizzy, and her teeth rotten and broken.

Oracus, you and Bandor must come with me," she ordered in her husky voice.

"Dyma, what's going on?" Garrin demanded. "I'm taking them to the palace."

"I have orders," Dyma reasoned. "They both must be imprisoned until Torvanon's return."

"Torvanon said nothing to me about this," Garrin contended.

"That's because he knew you'd disagree with his decision. After what Oracus did in Tallarin, it's best for everyone that he isn't granted freedom."

"But he didn't do anything in Tallarin!" Garrin argued.

"Garrin, it's fine," Oracus said, although he didn't really know why he was to be locked up. He nodded at Dyma. "I understand. Lead the way."

The guards quickly surrounded him and Bandor, and Dyma and Huadlan led them in the opposite direction of the palace. Garrin followed them all from behind, but Aquila took to the sky and left him alone.

Oracus and Bandor were escorted to a lone building with two floors and barred windows. Guards in green surrounded the building, which was grey stone rather than the yellow of the other structures nearby. When inside, Dyma showed Oracus along a corridor with dozens of cells either side, then up a narrow staircase. As they passed the cells, the prisoners protested their innocence.

The floor above was quieter than the one below, but more sinister. It was dark there, with little light to guide them. Eight steel doors lined that corridor of the jail, and Oracus realised he and Bandor would be imprisoned here to keep them more secure. As Dyma unlocked the two empty cells they would be occupying, Oracus listened to the thumps and grunts of what sounded like a man trying to headbutt his way to freedom.

"Please step inside," Dyma said as she slid the two doors open. When Oracus and Bandor were in their cells, she locked them, and then lifted the flap on Oracus's door. "You will remain here until Torvanon's return. If you attempt to escape, the guards will be forced to kill you."

The flap slammed shut and Dyma's footsteps retreated down the corridor with Huadlan's and her guards' close behind. Oracus felt a sinking feeling in his stomach.

"I thought the people here would be happier to see us," he said to Bandor.

There was a soft knock on the cell door and Garrin's voice spoke from behind it. "Do you want to talk?" he asked.

Oracus was glad Garrin had stayed in the jail because he had a lot of questions he wanted answering. "Yes, I do," he said. "Why am I in here?"

"They're saying you killed Catania in Tallarin and helped Jowra conquer the city," Garrin said. "You didn't, did you?"

The mention of his mother's name made a knot tighten in Oracus's chest. It had only been the evening before that he found the note and necklace in Emsbleek, and the feelings he had about it were still very raw. "I did kill her, but not to assist Jowra," he said honestly.

Garrin didn't immediately respond, but the sound of his leather gilet sliding down the metal door told Oracus he hadn't taken the news so well.

"Garrin?"

"You killed her?" The pain in his voice was clear.

"I had to," Oracus said glumly. "Jowra was controlling her and destroying the city from inside the palace."

"You didn't have to kill her though. Surely there was another way."

"If there had been, I would have done it," Oracus claimed. "She was my mother, Garrin. And Jowra's my grandfather. I found out almost the moment I arrived there."

Garrin was silent again for a while and Oracus sat with his back against the opposite side of the door. He put his head in his hands and wondered how his life had become so bad.

"That's why everyone here is worried," Garrin eventually said. "They've been saying you're Jowra's grandson and a Vassath Rider too. They think the two of you are going to rule Pharia together."

Oracus shook his head at the ridiculousness of it all. "I suppose it's Quent who's been spreading the lies?" he said.

"Quent didn't actually make it here. His group of evacuees got lost shortly after escaping Tallarin," Garrin explained. "But Dyma and Kivali have been spreading his lies for him."

Oracus's spirits suddenly rose. "Kivali's here?"

"Not right now. Her and Torvanon will hopefully be back in a day or two."

"Why, where are they?"

"On their way home from Fervia," Garrin said, and Oracus sensed uncertainty in his voice.

"What have they been to Fervia for?"

"Well, we attacked the city," Garrin said. "It was part of our plan to weaken Jowra. We had already destroyed Alvoria before Jowra sent his army to Tallarin, so Fervia was the next step."

"What happened?" Oracus probed. "Did you win?"

"Not exactly, but we didn't lose either," Garrin said. "They had more soldiers than we expected so it came as a shock at first. And they had Gravaz and Zarad waiting for us too. But it's what came at the end of the battle that worries me most."

Oracus was standing now and had pressed his ear against the door to hear Garrin clearly. "Go on," he urged.

"An army arrived from the oceans to the north, and because of the storm, they caught us by surprise."

"An army of Jowra's soldiers?"

"No, a different army. An army that killed as many of Jowra's men as our own."

"What kind of army?" Oracus pressured. But he already knew the answer to his own question. He had seen these creatures in his vision of King Xarmoud at the very end of the Noble War. He had been in Lalacia's library when it happened, and their black armour and pale faces had come at him with ferocious speed beneath storm clouds that flashed with lightning.

"It was an army of Fizorachis," Garrin confirmed.

TWENTY-ONE

Nivin

Garrin explained to Oracus what had happened in Fervia – from how they'd camped in the forest the night before the attack, to their flight when the Fizorachis came. By all accounts, it had been a massacre, with neither Jowra nor the rebellion claiming victory.

But the invasion of the Fizorachis brought with it uncertainty as well as death. Now Jowra had a war on two fronts to fight, as did the rebellion. But what was more, Gravaz was no longer a Rider, and Torvanon and Kivali still hadn't returned home. And Horvos had been killed by Zarad.

"I wish I hadn't left them," Garrin said. "Torvanon wanted me to fly back and warn everyone here. But what can we do? I should have stayed with them to help get the survivors back."

"Do you think they're okay?" Oracus asked.

"They're both tough but there's only two of them," he said. "I've thought about flying out to meet them but there's a lot of forest to search."

"And what of Gravaz?" Oracus quizzed.

"Gravaz? What does he matter?"

"Well, is he alive or dead?"

"I saw him being dragged away and that's about it. Fizorachis like to take captives and feed on their lives," he explained. "But he's not a Rider now so he doesn't concern us. As soon as Lapsin was killed, Gravaz lost his power. Besides, he'll never get out of a city full of Fizorachis."

Oracus bit his lip and wondered whether to share with Garrin why he was so keen to know if Gravaz was alive. At risk of sounding like a crazy prisoner, he knew he should keep his mouth shut, but he had always been honest with his friend, even as a child.

"Do you know why I was missing for a whole year?" he asked.

"According to some, you were playing cards with Jowra in his palace and discussing ways to rule," Garrin said with a laugh. "And Bandor was probably having a nice time wrestling Dragons."

Oracus smiled, but he was keen for Garrin to take him seriously. "I spent most of that time in the Black Forest," he said.

"The Black Forest?" Garrin repeated. "And you came out of there alive?"

"I was half-dead when I arrived there, Garrin. I was found by the Ulatoris and they helped me recover."

Garrin was silent once again. It seemed Oracus's adventures were taking him by surprise.

"Their leader is called Sarvon, and I agreed with him that I'd take Gravaz back to his village if he saved my life."

"And you intend to carry out your promise?" Garrin said. "Are you an idiot?"

"No, Garrin. I'm a man of my word."

"You have no reason to go to the Black Forest again," Garrin argued. "Why even bother? What will they do to you if you don't take Gravaz there? They haven't left the forest for decades. They won't come searching for you."

"I owe Sarvon my life and I will complete the task he entrusted me with!" Oracus said, feeling his temper beginning to rise. He wished he hadn't said anything to Garrin after all.

"So your plan is to what? Go to Fervia and rescue Gravaz, an Ulatori who has almost killed you twice before, and march him across Pharia to a bunch of savages who will probably celebrate his return?"

Jowra's fury spilled into Oracus's mind and an explosion of lightning erupted from his fingertips, bright and purple. The bang was loud and harsh, and a crack appeared in the wall to Oracus's left. As the echo died down, Jowra's anger died with it, and all Oracus was left with was a thumping heart.

The flap on the door opened and Garrin peered inside. "What are you doing in there?"

"Don't ever called them savages!" Oracus growled.

"If the rest of them are anything like Gravaz, then *savages* is exactly what they are," Garrin argued.

"You'd better leave now before I do something to you I can't control," Oracus said.

"Don't be like that," Garrin answered. His voice had softened, and Oracus wondered if he was feeling guilty or scared.

"Just leave me alone, Garrin. I don't want to talk to you anymore."

The flap snapped shut, and for a moment there was quiet. Oracus thought Garrin might try to apologise, but it was the sound of his retreating footsteps that came instead. Before long, there was silence except for the dull thud of the prisoner headbutting the wall.

"It was Jowra," Oracus said as Bandor soaked up the last of his anger. *"I could feel his temper again, and his power too this time."*

*

There were no lights in the jail, but Oracus could tell morning had arrived by the sounds of people in the streets outside. The walls of the prison were thick, but not thick enough to stop him hearing with Bandor's acute senses.

All night he had been sat in the corner of his cell, wide awake and confused. He had used one of Jowra's powers while arguing with Garrin the night before, even though the King was miles away in Melzor. He couldn't understand how, and he decided the only reasonable explanation was that Jowra's surge of anger must have caused it. Bandor thought the same, but was concerned by how easily Oracus was losing control, even when he was around the people he cared about.

Oracus felt trapped, both physically and mentally. And being alone in a cell was the last thing he needed. He should have been outside enjoying his freedom, where he could distract himself from thoughts of Jowra or his mother.

When he felt like he could take isolation no more, Oracus prepared himself to break out. He was sure Bandor would be able to knock down a wall or two. But before he'd started putting his plan into action, the flap on the door opened.

"'ello, Mr Oracus?" a quiet voice asked.

Curious as to who was speaking, Oracus looked through the flap and saw a skinny young boy standing in the dark corridor. The boy looked very much like a mouse. He was small and shy, with big hazel eyes and a pointy nose. He had freckles too, and messy brown hair that covered his ears. The boy looked very timid, with his bare toes pigeoned and one hand clasping the other in front of his belly.

"Who are you?" Oracus asked.

The boy shuffled towards him and didn't lift his eyes from the floor. "Am Nivin, Sir."

"How did you get past the guards, Nivin?"

The boy raised his gaze and a guilty smile crossed his face. He looked even more like a mouse then, for his front teeth had overlapped his bottom lip. "I sneaked in ter see yer, Sir," he whispered proudly.

Nivin's accent reminded Oracus of some of the poorer folk in Tallarin. And seeing his large clothes with rolled-up sleeves and trouser-legs made him wonder if Nivin was indeed a refugee. "Are you from Tallarin?" he asked.

"Tha' I am, Sir," he answered. "I were brought 'ere after the battle wi' Jowra's men."

"I thought as much," Oracus said. "But why are you here looking for me?"

"Me father said yer a good man, Sir," Nivin said with a bow. "Din't talk o' owt else whenever 'e came 'ome from 'is travels."

"Who is your father?" Oracus enquired interestedly.

"Morpac, Sir."

"I knew your father quite well. I could say many nice things about him too."

Nivin beamed. "Well, 'e told me yer rescued 'im from captivity by killin' a thousand Grevlors and Lisors in a cave in the mountains!" He flailed his arms around as if he was holding a sword and slaying Grevlors and Lisors in that very corridor.

"Impressive," Oracus observed. He had indeed saved Morpac and his friend Uswir from a group of Jowra's servants in the mountains. And the two men had gifted him with the elegant dagger on his belt as a thank-you. "Does your father know you're here?"

"'e's dead, Sir. Was killed wi' the rest o' me family back 'ome." Nivin looked ruefully at the floor again.

"I'm sorry to hear that," Oracus said. It was hard to hear that the war had claimed another good man. And left a son fatherless too.

"Tha's okay," Nivin replied. "Mr Oracus, I came up 'ere ter ask yer summin' importan' though."

"Go ahead," Oracus urged.

"Well, me father thought a lot o' yer," Nivin started. "But there's rumours yer in 'ere 'cause yer on Jowra's side. Is tha' true?"

"No, those rumours are false," Oracus said quickly.

"Good," Nivin replied, a huge grin spreading across his face. "I never believed 'em anyway."

"Is that what you came here for? To ask me that?"

"Not jus' tha'," he replied. "I thought yer migh' like some 'elp gettin' out. I'm very good at pickin' locks!"

Nivin held up a length of wire and Oracus stared at him in disbelief. Suddenly, he felt guilty for planning to escape the jail only a few minutes prior. It wouldn't be setting a very good example to boys like Nivin. "Before you came here, I was considering breaking myself out because I was lonely," Oracus admitted. "But now you've come to talk to me, I feel much better. Imagine how much trouble I would have been in if you hadn't arrived."

Nivin was so proud of himself his face glowed red. But he quickly slipped the wire back inside his shirt.

"In the future," Oracus said, lowering his voice and ushering Nivin nearer, "don't offer to help anyone escape prison."

"I wouldn' 'elp jus' anyone, Sir," Nivin claimed. "Only you."

"Not even me. Do you understand?"

Nivin nodded and his brown eyes lowered to the floor again. Then he snapped them upwards and looked excited all of a sudden. "Any chance I can see yer Lavorian?" he whispered.

"Sure," Oracus granted. "He's in the next cell over."

Nivin skipped away from Oracus's door and opened the flap on Bandor's cell with a bang.

Next second, "Wow! 'e's enormous! 'is 'ead almos' touches the ceilin'! Can I touch 'im, Mr Oracus? Please?"

"I can talk, you know," Bandor said before Oracus could respond.

There was a loud thud, and Oracus guessed Nivin had fallen over in shock. He looked through the flap and saw the boy getting back to his feet. "He is enormous. But I think you should get out of here now before someone hears you."

Nivin looked disappointed. "Bu' canna come back an' see yer again?"

"Of course. And if I'm released, you can see me on the outside and you won't have to sneak past any guards to talk to me."

His words made Nivin jump with delight. "I guess al see yer soon then," he said enthusiastically. Then he tottered happily to the stairs, whistling as he went, and jumped out of sight.

"He was a very unusual child," Bandor said simply, making Oracus laugh.

"It's nice to meet someone who's happy to see us for a change," Oracus said. *"But forget about that, I have better news!"*

"What is it?"

"Torvanon and Kivali's minds reached mine while Nivin was here. They're alive and back home!"

"That's great," Bandor agreed. *"And with any luck, Torvanon will come straight here to let us out."*

Twenty-Two

Old Friend, New Friend

Indeed, Torvanon did attend the prison almost immediately. But the happy, jovial Torvanon Oracus had befriended during his last visit to Afarra was absent. Instead, the leader was grouchy and sullen, with pallid skin and bloodshot eyes. He looked like he hadn't slept in days, and Oracus supposed he would have been the same given similar circumstances. Horvos, his closest friend, had been killed in front of him, then he'd seen his army halved when the Fizorachis invaded.

"I must say I'm surprised you're alive," Torvanon said when Oracus finished explaining where he'd been since Tallarin. "We all thought we'd never see you again."

"I feel lucky to be here," Oracus admitted. "But I'm not sure why I'm still locked up. It's understandable that you doubted me before, but everything I've done is to end Jowra's reign, not support it."

"You killed Catania," Torvanon said. "Surely you can understand our reservations about you."

"You still don't trust me, do you? Even after everything I've told you," Oracus claimed. "Jowra killed my father and forced me to kill my mother. Why would I betray you to join him?"

"I did think he might have brainwashed you when Kivali first told me what you did, but not now," Torvanon said with a shake of his head. "However, you have been with the Ulatoris for a year. And that in itself is unusual. It's something Jowra did himself half a century ago."

"They're as against Jowra as we are."

"That maybe so, but it's also well-known how much they hate Humans. How do I know you haven't been sent here by them to kill us all?"

Oracus rolled his eyes. "You can't be serious?"

Torvanon shrugged his shoulders. He seemed a lot less the leader he had been once. He was void of confidence and joy.

"Are you going to let me out of here, or not?" Oracus asked impatiently.

"We stand little chance against Jowra *and* the Fizorachis anyway, let alone without you," Torvanon said. "And if it turns out you're fighting for Jowra or the Ulatoris then at least we'll all be put out our misery sooner."

"I thought your reason for freeing me would be because you trust me, not because you have no choice."

Torvanon shrugged again. "It is what it is, Oracus."

And with that, he exited the cell and left the door open. Oracus waited for a moment, then walked out onto the corridor, where Bandor was already waiting for him. *"Do you get the feeling we don't belong anywhere anymore?"* he said to Bandor.

They left the prison and a fresh autumn breeze carried orange leaves along the streets. The fading sun was dropping over the city buildings as evening closed in, yet there was still a pleasant warmth in the air. Oracus made the most of his time alone with Bandor and took a stroll around the city that would end at the cemetery where his father was buried. The city was unusually quiet, and nobody bothered them as they walked. Oracus remembered when Bandor was still a cub, and he would hide him in his shirt whenever he took to these streets. Back then, the people would have swarmed around a Rider and Lavorian, but today they showed little interest. Oracus didn't mind, for he was able to enjoy the peace, but it was a stark warning of how the war was making people feel.

After an hour, Oracus and Bandor finally reached the cemetery, where the old gravestones spanned far and wide. There were wreaths and bunches of flowers on many of the graves, as well as crisp leaves from the oak trees that had recently been shed. Oracus noticed wind chimes dangling from some gravestones too, offering a tranquil melody to the emptiness.

When Oracus reached his father's resting place, it was a strange feeling. He sat between Bandor's front legs and closed his eyes, trying for the first time in a while to remember what his father looked like. The eyes were easy, for they were the same green as his own, but the shape of his nose and the sound of his voice had been lost to time. It was sad that the events of the last year had forced him to forget.

For long into the night, Oracus stayed with Bandor beside his father's grave. He had nowhere to sleep for the night, so intended to stay in the cemetery. It was his wish for Bandor to withdraw all his senses too; it was more peaceful in the darkness and silence.

Throughout the long hours, Oracus cried a few times, like he had done more than once recently. But it wasn't just the loss of his father and the note from his mother that made him sad, it was the lack of hope amongst the rebellion too. He had often wondered during his absence whether Afarra had fallen after Tallarin's defeat. He didn't, however, expect the people to be resigned to defeat, despite the city still standing strong.

"Oracus." Bandor's voice made him jump. The Lavorian had been asleep, so Oracus had heard nothing more than his gentle snores for some time. *"There's someone behind us. They're lingering in the shadows."*

"I know you're there," Oracus said aloud. As soon as he spoke, Bandor restored his senses and the sound of crunching leaves could be heard.

"It's just me." Kivali's voice was unmistakeable, even after months without hearing it.

"What are you doing here?" Oracus asked her without turning around.

"I heard you were back," she said. "I went to see you in the prison but Torvanon had already released you."

Oracus stood up and looked at her. He was angry for a second, but when he saw her face, the anger subsided. She was just as beautiful as always, with blue eyes like pools of water Oracus wanted to dive into. She was thinner than she had been, gaunt even, but it did nothing to soften her glow. "Why would you want to see *me*?" he asked her. "You think I work for Jowra, don't you?"

Kivali eyed him seriously but didn't retaliate. "I missed you actually."

"You missed me so much that you told everyone in Afarra I'm working for him."

"I was hurting!" she exclaimed. "I opened up to you in Tallarin like I never have before. Then you killed Catania and the city fell. When Quent told me what you'd done, you weren't there to explain yourself. You disappeared!"

Oracus laughed at the sound of Quent's name. "I was blasted into the ocean by Gravaz after your beloved Quent left me to die," he said.

"I had no reason to disbelieve him," Kivali claimed.

"Do you still believe him now?"

"He must have made a mistake. I've had a long time to think about it and of course I know you aren't on Jowra's side."

"Quent refused when I asked for his help. And he lied to you about what he'd seen in Catania's palace," Oracus argued. "And where do you think he is now? Probably laughing about it in Melzor."

"The group of evacuees he left Tallarin with went missing," Kivali said. "He's probably dead and you're speaking ill of him. He's not a bad person and he certainly doesn't work for Jowra."

"When you thought I was dead, you were happy to hear Quent speak ill of me," Oracus said. "But now you're jumping to his defence when all the evidence points to him."

Kivali shook her head. "It's not like that, Oracus, I promise you."

"Well it sure sounds like it," he said. "I came here to remember my father in peace and I didn't want to be disturbed. Least of all by you." He flashed Kivali a fierce look and placed his hand on Bandor's leg. Using Kivali's power, he teleported them away from the cemetery and into the small room where his father had died. It was the first place that had come to his mind.

The room was how exactly how he'd left it all those months ago, but with more dust. The bed was still against the wall and dressed in the same sheets, and the window still looked out over the marketplace below.

Oracus sat on the bed and began to regret how he'd spoken to Kivali. *"I shouldn't have said those things to her,"* he said. *"I have too few friends as it is."*

Bandor lay down because he was so big now that his head was as high as the ceiling. *"I think it was important for you to be honest with her. It would have been worse if you'd lied and pretended not to be upset,"* he said. *"But maybe you shouldn't have just vanished."*

"I felt Jowra's anger creeping up on me again. I needed to get away from her."

"You're going to have to talk to somebody about that," Bandor said with concern. *"Maybe there's a way to stop him getting into your mind."*

Oracus doubted anyone in Afarra could help him, and the thought of discussing his visions was an ominous one. Especially with everybody already treating him like a criminal.

He placed his sword and necklace on the wooden floor, then removed the armour and underclothes he hadn't changed out of since his travels. When he lay down on the bed, he thanked the stars for guiding him to Afarra safely, and thanked fate for granting him his freedom. Finally, when sleep offered to embrace him, he made a promise to himself not to push away any more of his friends.

*

A light tap on the shoulder woke Oracus early the next morning. He slowly opened his eyes to daylight, but jerked awake upon realising a huge pair of brown eyes were staring down at him.

"Mornin', sir!"

Oracus screamed and scampered backwards, banging his head on the wall in the process. "Nivin!" he yelled. "What are you doing here?"

"Sorry, Sir. I din't mean ter scare yer," Nivin muttered apologetically. "I were jus' enjoyin' watchin' yer sleep!"

"Don't ever do that again!" Oracus exclaimed. "You scared me half to death."

"I said I were sorry, Mr Oracus." He stepped back and sniffed sadly.

Oracus breathed heavily and forced himself to calm down. "It's fine. How long have you been here?"

"Quite a while," the boy answered. "Did yer know that you're nude?"

Oracus quickly covered his dignity with a hand, then got up to retrieve his underclothes. "No, I forgot. Thank you." As he pulled on his shorts, he looked at Bandor. *"Did you know he was in here standing over me?"*

Bandor had stirred at Oracus's scream, but made no move to defend him. *"No, I didn't,"* he admitted.

"You're supposed to protect me!" Oracus claimed.

"Well I didn't hear him come in," Bandor said innocently. *"What was I supposed to do?"*

Oracus rolled his eyes and turned back to Nivin. "How did you know I was here?" he asked.

"Just a lucky guess," Nivin replied, shrugging his narrow shoulders.

Oracus frowned. “A lucky guess?” he repeated. “So, of all the houses you could have broken into to find me, you happened to choose this one?”

Nivin nodded. “Yes, Sir.”

“And you opened the door, climbed the staircase, then crept over here without waking my Lavorian?”

“Yes, Sir,” Nivin said again.

“How?” Oracus asked, stunned.

“Well, I tiptoed,” Nivin answered, shrugging once more.

Oracus opened and closed his mouth. He’d only just woke up and his brain was struggling to comprehend what was going on. "Why are you here?”

“Yer said I could visit yer whenever I wan’ed ter when yer’d bin released.”

“How did you know I’d been released?”

“I jus’ did,” Nivin said cheerily, oblivious to Oracus’s confusion.

“Well, did you see me leave the prison?” Oracus asked.

“No, Sir.”

“Did you hear from somebody else that I’d been let out?”

“No, Sir.”

“So you just… *knew*?”

“Yes, Sir.”

Oracus was in danger of getting a headache. With his clothes now donned, he sat back on the bed and put his head in his hands. “Are you visiting me for any particular reason, Nivin?”

“Not really, Sir,” the boy said. Then his big eyes widened at a sudden thought. “Bu’ I would like ter learn ‘ow ter fight. Any chance yer could teach me? Me father always said yer were an excellen’ fighter.”

Oracus thought for a moment. "Sorry, I can't right now. I haven't eaten."

As if he'd been expecting that exact response, Nivin pulled an apple from the breast pocket of his oversized shirt. He rubbed it clean on his trousers and passed it to Oracus. "Tha'll keep yer goin', Sir."

Oracus took the apple and cursed himself for using such a poor excuse. "Alright then," he said, taking a bite. "Let's go now. I was going to train anyway."

Bandor stayed behind to sleep while Oracus guided Nivin to the training area outside Torvanon's palace. It was so early that dew was glistening in the meadow adjacent, and the target range was still deep in the palace's shadow. Oracus had expected to see soldiers sparring given the height of the war, but not a soul was there. Maybe the return of many exhausted men from Fervia the day before was the reason.

"Me father 'ad all these weapons in 'is workshop back 'ome," Nivin said as he studied the full weapon rack. "'e never let me touch a single one, though. 'e said they were far too dangerous."

The revelation made Oracus uncomfortable. He had respected Morpac greatly, and if the man from Tallarin had warned his son about weapons, Oracus wasn't willing to teach him how to fight with one. He was happy for the boy to look, but when Nivin tried with all his might to pull the biggest war axe off the rack, he was forced to intervene. "Leave it alone before you hurt yourself," he said.

Nivin frowned but obliged.

"I am so good with a sword now because I learned to fight with my fists before wielding one. My advice would be the same to you."

"So I can't use a weapon at all?"

"When you can fight effectively with your fists, I will allow you to choose any weapon you like."

The look on Nivin's face resembled Oracus's expression when Sarvon had spoken the same words to him under Iniril.

"Do you trust me to make you a good fighter?" Oracus asked him.

Nivin nodded, so for the next hour, Oracus taught him some of the basics of fighting. He showed him the correct fighting stance, the best way to dodge attacks, how to counter attacks, and the weak spots on an opponent's body for him to punch and kick. Nivin enjoyed the training, having soon forgotten his eagerness to grab a weapon, and Oracus felt happier too. It made a nice change to be teaching instead of being taught.

Eventually, when Nivin's baggy clothes were soaked in sweat, Oracus ended the session. Nivin slumped to the floor and rubbed his shoulders, but was smiling nonetheless.

"You did really well!" Oracus said. "I'm really impressed."

Nivin beamed ever more, and then a thunderous applause came from one man who had been watching from the palace.

"Bravo! Bravo!"

It was Karvan the fight trainer, the strong, bearded man from Thessley. He strode towards them with his chest bare and his arms outstretched.

"It's great to see you back! I was afraid you hadn't survived." He grasped Oracus in a bone-crunching hug. When he released him, he knelt beside Nivin and ruffled the boy's hair. "That was some fighting, young man. You'll make a fine soldier one day."

Nivin's freckly face lifted and he offered Karvan a toothy grin.

"You're training youngsters now?" Karvan said, standing up and looking back at Oracus.

"Only this once. He wanted to learn," Oracus said. "It's wonderful to see you again, Karvan."

Karvan pulled him into a second hug and the hairs on his chest tickled Oracus's face. When Oracus looked up at him, there was a tear in the big man's eye.

"Are you still teaching?" Oracus asked when he was allowed to step back.

"Torvanon made me one of the lead trainers here," Karvan answered, wiping his cheek. "It's nice to be able to help out, you know. Some of the men survived in Fervia because of my lessons, and that makes me really proud."

"Did you travel to Fervia with them?"

"No, thank goodness. Torvanon left me here to keep training those who had been left behind."

"Are there many soldiers still alive?" Oracus asked.

"Well, we lost a lot in Fervia, Oracus. And I mean *a lot*. Half of those who were trying to flee the battlefield were slaughtered by the Fizorachis." Karvan paused and looked out across the meadow. "Including all the students and those from Tallarin who weren't fit to invade Fervia, maybe we have five-thousand who can fight. Nowhere near enough to stop Jowra if he decided to attack."

"Do you think he will attack? Even after what happened in Fervia?"

"I have no idea," Karvan admitted. "I thought he would have come here the moment Tallarin fell. For some reason, he decided not to."

"That surprises me too," Oracus agreed. "I wasn't expecting Afarra to be standing when I arrived."

"I bet you weren't expecting to be locked up when you arrived either."

"No, I wasn't," Oracus said. "Did *you* think I was serving the King?"

Karvan smiled warmly and placed a hairy hand on Oracus's shoulder. "I've known you all your life. I've never doubted you for one second."

The simple gesture of support was a huge relief to Oracus and it made him the happiest he'd felt for some time.

"It's been playing on your mind, hasn't it?" Karvan said wisely. When Oracus bowed his head, he continued. "People will say and believe all sorts when they're scared. I know how much you loved your father, so I know you would never join the man who brought about his death. Unfortunately, nobody else sees the bigger picture. Everyone was just looking for someone to blame and you were an easy target because you weren't there."

"If everyone in the land except those closest to me didn't trust me, then I wouldn't care," Oracus explained. "But those with whom I've shared my deepest secrets are questioning my actions like I had a choice. It's not fair."

"I understand why that makes you upset, but now you're home and can prove them all wrong. Hold a grudge if you must, but that won't win us this war. What we need now is a sense of unity."

As much as it pained Oracus to hear, he knew Karvan was right. He needed to apologise to Garrin, Kivali and Torvanon, and then help them to trust him again. If they were going to bring Jowra down together, he needed them on his side immediately.

Oracus nodded his head gratefully at Karvan and then started towards the palace. "Shall we go and see Torvanon now then?" he said. "I'll arrange a council meeting with him for first thing tomorrow morning."

Twenty-Three

Revisiting The Past

Hate, fury, and the desire to kill bubbled within Jowra like never before. He yelled so loudly that the walls rattled, and his Dragons cowered in the corner of the keep, desperate to evade his rage. The flames in the lamps blew out, and even the stars high above the open ceiling seemed to lose their twinkle, afraid that casting too much light upon the King might cause him to destroy them.

The vehemence of his anger built until a violent tempest began to encircle him and bolts of lightning erupted from his fingertips. Huge chunks of black stone began to fall away from the walls, and he could feel the palace creaking under his immense power. He was in half a mind to rip it from its foundations and leave nothing more than a giant pile of rubble, just like he'd done to the palace in Tallarin. Destruction was the only way he would ever quench the boiling animosity inside, but he resisted the urge and reduced the roaring storm to nothing.

Jowra brushed his black hair out of his face and paced back and forth, questioning himself, deciding how best to proceed. Loose stone tumbled from high above and smashed on the floor, but he ignored it while he procrastinated. His army had fallen in Fervia, not to the rebellion, but to the race in black who had invaded from the northern shore. They were called Fizorachis; he had read about them in the tomes and texts in his collection. But he hadn't foreseen their surprise attack.

He would have to send another army to north-east to banish them, he determined. But before he risked more men, he would need to speak to someone who knew first-hand what the Fizorachis were capable of.

Jowra calmed himself and the Dragons slithered out of their corner. As they wrapped their enormous bodies around him, he forced his mind into Gravaz's head and took possession of the Ulatori's body. He was no longer in the keep, but in a tiny, dark room with a stone bed and the smallest barred window that overlooked a desolate Fervia that was shrouded by storm clouds. Looking down at himself, he noticed his muscular grey body was bare, and his skin was covered in the same grime that coated the surrounding walls.

"You have failed me, Gravaz," Jowra whispered clearly inside his minion's head.

Gravaz shuddered at the sound of his master's voice. "I'm sorry, my King," he replied.

"But I do not feel your remorse," Jowra tested. "And neither do I feel your regret."

"Forgive me, my King, but at this time I feel nothing except sorrow." His voice was deep, but empty. And his words were not spoken with the hunger they once had been.

"You swore to be my loyal servant in return for your life," Jowra stated. "Yet you carelessly handed over my city to worthless invaders without trying to stop them!"

"I did all I could," Gravaz said plainly.

"Do not speak to me like I am a common fool!" Jowra spat. "I am the King of Pharia and I will not give hope to these parasites from another land."

"There is nothing you can do," Gravaz said.

"Nothing I can do?" Jowra repeated loudly, angrily. "Nothing that I, King Jowra, the most powerful King Pharia has ever seen, can do about these foul creatures who kill my men and aim to plunder my cities?"

"They have not just come to plunder your cities, my King," Gravaz said, the tone of his voice unchanged. "They wish to conquer Pharia and feast upon the abundance of life here."

"Ha! They will never conquer Pharia!" Jowra expressed. "I will murder them all now whilst I reside within your weak and insignificant body!"

Now had come the time for Jowra to discharge his fury and *destroy*. He would rip down the door, tear out the window and smash the walls of this feeble holding. He would slaughter the race in black for daring to take what was his. He raised his enormous grey hands and pointed them towards the door, ready to cause devastation, ready to smell blood in the air...

But he couldn't do it. There was something holding back his powers; an invisible force he'd never felt before. And it was mighty enough to saturate him.

"What is happening?" he yelled incredulously, looking down at Gravaz's hands.

"Your powers will not work here, my King," the Ulatori explained simply.

"What do you mean?" Jowra asked. The anxiety in his voice was apparent now, despite his efforts to contain it.

"The Fizorachis are surrounding this prison, and you cannot use your powers when they are near."

Jowra roared with displeasure. "Then you are useless to me! I should just kill you now," he cried.

"Please do," Gravaz said. "I have lost my Lavorian. There is nothing I care for anymore."

"Then I will leave you to rot in that cell!" Jowra bellowed. He withdrew from Gravaz's body and was inside the keep once more. The veins in his head throbbed dangerously and his eyes glowed scarlet. The winds started again, and they soon developed into a cyclone that crumbled the palace walls. His fury was uncontrollable now, and his fear was growing significantly. He hadn't felt so powerless since the day his mother and sisters had died.

*

Oracus sat upright in his bed and breathed deeply, like he'd reached the surface after a long time underwater. It took a moment for the anger to subside and for him to realise he wasn't in Melzor. It had been a dream, and he was actually safe in Afarra.

He lay back down on the bed where his father had died and rolled over to look at Bandor. The Lion was already awake and watching him. *"It was Jowra again,"* he said.

"I thought as much," Bandor replied. *"I tried to wake you but I couldn't. How do you feel?"*

"I'm fine," Oracus said. He took another deep breath. *"I just can't shut him out."*

"What happened in your dream?"

"Jowra's found out the Fizorachis invaded. He knows he's lost Fervia," Oracus explained.

"I doubt he's happy about that."

"No, he isn't," Oracus confirmed. *"But Gravaz is alive, Bandor. Jowra possessed his body like he did to my mother in Tallarin."*

"He's still in Fervia?"

"He's locked in the same prison I was in. The Fizorachis must be feeding off him like Garrin said they would."

"Do you want to go there and get him out?"

"I don't want to but it's necessary," Oracus said. *"I promised Sarvon we'd deliver him to them so we have no choice."*

"And how are we going to get Gravaz out once we're inside Fervia? You won't be able to use your powers there."

"I haven't planned that far ahead," Oracus said truthfully. He looked out the window and saw a clear blue sky. *"But I've got that meeting with Torvanon and the others now in the council room. We can discuss the logistics of a rescue mission later."*

Oracus got up and dressed himself, then looked down on the busy market below. The people of Afarra appeared active this morning, and he wasn't much in the mood for being glared at.

"I don't want to walk through all those people. I think I'll just teleport to the palace," he said, running his fingers through Bandor's mane. *"Stay in my mind and I'll be back soon."*

The dusty room quickly disappeared as Oracus teleported, and it was replaced by the colourful courtyard that preceded the glorious palace. On either side of a central path, luscious green lawns soaked up the hot sun, as did the hedgerows and flowerbeds that surrounded them. Oracus was surprised to see several Sashtrams from Tallarin around the courtyard, although it seemed obvious upon consideration that they would have been evacuated with the rest of the people from the fallen city. They were short, blue creatures with odd habits and a knack for clumsiness. Sashtrams weren't unlike the Azzeils of Malum, yet they were much friendlier. They were happy and smiley and round, not sharp-toothed and sinister. The people who relaxed and picnicked on the lawns watched the Sashtrams curiously as they cleaned and gardened. One was even on his hands and knees, trimming individual blades of grass with a tiny pair of scissors.

At the end of the courtyard, a large, stone archway curved over the path, and Oracus passed through it and climbed the palace steps. Above him, the palace stood proud, four square tiers of it stood one on top of the other. From the parapet of the first tier, archers observed the courtyard with watchful eyes.

At the top of the stone steps, two sentries with spears guarded the polished oak doors. When Oracus approached, they stepped aside, and he passed through into the entrance hall beyond.

The foyer was exactly as Oracus remembered it. The walls were green and gold, and the floor black and white marble. All around were stone columns that propped the high ceiling and doors that led to different rooms of the palace. Directly ahead, two grand staircases arched up to a guarded terrace above.

A second set of oak doors was what Oracus passed through next. This was the feast hall where he'd first met Torvanon. There were ten long tables that stretched almost the length of the room, and a high table placed perpendicular to them. The tables were already dressed for the evening feast, with hundreds of crockery and cutlery sets laid out perfectly. Oracus crossed the room, passing under a ceiling festooned with gold and green banners, to reach yet another door that led to the sultry council room.

A wooden table was already occupied by seven in a room barely able to fit five. Torvanon, Garrin and Karvan were sat on one side of the table, with a spare chair for Oracus, while Kivali, Dyma, Farlog and Croij occupied the seats on the other side. On entry, Oracus was welcomed with smiles by most, yet Torvanon and Dyma offered him nothing. Torvanon had lost all control of his hair and beard, and his eyes were sunken and dark. It seemed the death of Horvos had hit him hard, and the effects of the war were taking their toll. Dyma had also lost control of her hair, but that's how it had always been. The reason she didn't welcome Oracus was probably because she didn't trust him.

Farlog and Croij looked just as they had in Tallarin. Silver-haired, tall, wizened, and identical in every way. Oracus was pleased to see them well, despite their third brother having lost his life in Tallarin. He held out a hand for them both to shake, then took to his seat.

"Now we're all here, shall we get on with the meeting?" Torvanon said seriously. He looked around at them all, his eyes even darker in a room so lacking in light. "I understand everyone is now up to date with the events of the last few months?" He glanced at Oracus for a moment, who gave a brief nod. "It has been our task to weaken Jowra before ultimately ending his reign. So far, we have destroyed Alvoria and watched Fervia fall to the Fizorachis. During the latter, both the King and the rebellion lost a considerable number of soldiers. Admittedly, it has weakened us, but not as significantly as it has weakened him. If ever there was a time to be optimistic during great loss, now would be it."

There was silence in the room for a minute, and Oracus's thoughts fell on Horvos, who he knew would have revelled in a meeting like this.

"So what's the next step in the plan?" Farlog eventually asked. He leaned forwards and touched his fingertips together beneath his chin.

"Jowra has three cities remaining," Garrin said. "Lalacia, Malum and Melzor."

"Lalacia is a trading city," Kivali said. "There's no need to send soldiers there."

"So that leaves Malum and Melzor," Karvan deduced. "Are we to attack Malum before we face Jowra?"

Torvanon scratched at his tangled beard. "We would have to march past Melzor to get there," he said.

"Which would suggest a journey there would be unnecessary too," Croij concluded.

"Unless there's something in Malum worth making the journey for," Torvanon said. "I understand Oracus visited the city not too long ago."

"No surprise there," Dyma muttered under her breath.

Oracus chose to ignore her. "I'm not sure what you'd attack Malum for. Jowra doesn't have any troops there, just a Rider and who-knows-how-many Azzeils. Destroying the city wouldn't really affect him."

"Did you not say that several thousand prisoners are being held there beneath the palace?" Torvanon asked.

Oracus's mouth dropped open in realisation.

"Thousands of prisoners who have probably done nothing wrong and would take great pleasure in helping us bring about Jowra's downfall," Torvanon added.

"You're right," Oracus agreed. "Except most of them looked old and dying. Like they'd been there for years."

"A spell, most likely," Farlog said. "It's my understanding the Rider there is quite the master of disguise, is she not?"

"You know of Xintora?" Oracus asked.

"She's a Hazinal. The only one left, to our knowledge. Although I suspect some may still be existing *outside* our knowledge."

The thought made Oracus shiver. He imagined enjoying the company of someone who looked like Xintora, when really they looked like the scaly green creature she had become during his escape.

"It would be my best guess that many of those prisoners are strong soldiers, hunters and scouts being weakened by magic," Farlog concluded.

"Those men would be quite an addition to an army set for Melzor," Karvan said. "It's certainly worth considering how we can free them."

"I think I know a way," Oracus started. But Dyma scraped back her chair and stood up.

"I'm sorry. But am I the only one here concerned about Jowra being passed these plans?" she said.

Oracus rounded on her. "I assume you're talking about me passing them on?" he said sharply.

"Well Quent did warn us all about you," she answered.

"So I've been told!" Oracus said irritably. "And I'm getting tired of hearing his accusations from other people. I'd much prefer to hear them from him, but he's *missing*."

"Oracus, we've talked about this. You know we all trust you," Kivali tried to assure.

"No, I'm going to clear this up once and for all. I am not on Jowra's side! It was my Visioning that warned everybody of his attack on Tallarin in the first place. Then it was me who killed Catania, my own mother, to stop him tearing down the city and killing everyone in it. Now I'm having visions of him every night so I could probably tell you all his plans without you risking a single scout." Oracus took a deep breath and continued. "Furthermore, I have a way of obtaining the prisoners in Malum without sending any soldiers there."

The group went quiet, including Dyma. Oracus caught Garrin smiling, and he saw a glimmer in Torvanon's eye that had been missing since his return from Fervia.

"What I was going to say before being interrupted was that I am close to forming an alliance with, what would be, a very valuable group of people."

"What people?" Croij prompted impatiently.

"I was captured after Tallarin by the Ulatoris of the Black Forest. Before they killed me, they offered me a deal. A deal I accepted and one I am expected to keep."

Garrin's smile had vanished already. It seemed he still felt the same about Oracus preparing to risk his life for a promise to the Ulatoris.

"For sparing my life, they want me to return Gravaz to them." Oracus looked at them all seriously to show he wasn't joking. "The Ulatoris despise Jowra, and I believe they would assist us if I showed them I was trustworthy. They live two days south of Malum, and they wouldn't have to compromise themselves by marching past Melzor to get there."

"Your first problem is that Gravaz is likely dead already," Kivali said.

"I had a vision of Jowra just last night," Oracus answered. "And Gravaz was very much alive when Jowra entered his mind."

"A second issue is where the prisoners will go after the Ulatoris free them – if the Ulatoris *agree* to free them, that is," Croij added.

"I think I have a solution to that, but I need to think it over first," Oracus said. "But more importantly, I need to be able to enter Fervia to free Gravaz from the Fizorachis. They drain a Rider's powers, do they not?"

"They do," Torvanon confirmed. "I've had first-hand experience of it."

"I'm going to need some time to organise a plan," Oracus said. "And to solve those two problems, I'll need to meet with Farlog and Croij alone. There are questions I have only they will know the answer to."

"You'll need my permission to leave too," Torvanon said. "The last time you left this city, you almost died more than once."

Oracus turned to him and smiled. "Without the Ulatoris or prisoners in Malum to bolster our ranks, you know this war cannot be won. If we're to stand any chance of victory, you need to let me go."

Torvanon rubbed his chin thoughtfully. "If you cannot provide me with a solid plan in a week, I will return you to the prison and have Ursus guard the door so you can't escape." He looked serious, but the redness had returned to his cheeks. He wasn't so filled with grief now there was talk of victory.

"I'll prove to you all that I'm on the side of the rebels," Oracus said. He looked at Torvanon then. "I won't let you down."

TWENTY-FOUR

The Wise And The Inventive

Following the meeting in the council room, Oracus enjoyed a feeling of togetherness and friendship he had long forgotten. It appeared he had convinced those who had doubted him since Tallarin's defeat to trust him. And he finally felt like he was embracing the war, rather than trying to adapt to it.

Oracus spent the rest of the day with Garrin and Kivali by the ocean, where the dormant apples trees swayed almost leafless in the breeze. They skimmed stones on the water and raced their Lavorians over grass and sand, between telling stories of their lives during better times. It was nice to experience normality again for once, instead of feeling the constant pressure of being a Rider searching for victory in a land rife with conflict.

Finding time to reminisce about sweet childhood memories in Thessley was a form of much needed therapy, Oracus realised. Telling his friends of the summer days on the farm with his father was quite satisfying, as was recalling the many hours he spent tracking game through the forest. It was odd, too, hearing Garrin recount stories of their mischievous adolescence. Like the time they stole a dead pig from Broid the butcher in the middle of the night, only to find out it wasn't dead, and in fact sleeping. The cursed beast squealed and squealed until the entire village was awake, and when they were caught, they were both forced to stuff sausages for a week as punishment.

But even since becoming a Rider, Oracus had found places that brought him peace. He remembered the mushroom fountain in Lalacia where the fireflies gathered, and it would take a lifetime to forget how breath-taking Iniril had been. He even thought about the tranquil aroma in Shurgda's hut, and wondered if the Ulatori healer had thought about him since he'd left.

After a long day of fun and relaxation, Oracus returned to the house where his father had died. For the rest of the afternoon, he scrubbed the rooms from top to bottom, clearing them of all their dust and cobwebs. Then he laid on the bed and regarded his handiwork.

"You're quiet," he said to Bandor. For the whole time he was cleaning, the Lion had watched him. But now he had his head on his paws, purring sleepily.

"I'm really tired," he replied with a yawn that bared his silver teeth.

Oracus rolled off the bed and leaned against Bandor's side. He considered the day he'd had, and how much joy it had brought him. *"Who'd have thought we'd be looking to leave the city again so soon,"* he said.

"We don't have to go straight away," Bandor said. *"We can stay longer if you want."*

"No, we should go as soon as possible. The longer we wait, the further the Fizorachis will have spread, and the harder it will be to find Gravaz."

"You have to speak to Farlog and Croij first," Bandor reminded. *"They might say saving Gravaz is impossible, and then we'll have to re-evaluate."*

Oracus pushed himself to his feet. *"I'd better go and see them now before the feast. Are you coming?"*

"No, I'll stay here and sleep. The corridors in that palace are too narrow. And I can barely squeeze through the doors either these days."

Oracus scratched Bandor's chin. *"I won't be long,"* he said. Then he focused his power and teleported to the foyer of the palace.

As Oracus arrived, he was met by a Sashtram who screamed at his sudden arrival. That in turn frightened another Sashtram, who dropped a glass water jug that smashed on the marble floor. Oracus briefly apologised, then teleported onward, not wanting to involve himself in the clean-up.

He came to the top of a flight of stairs next, in a corridor full of portraits. He was in the third tier of the palace, and looking through the window gave him a beautiful view of the city. The courtyard was down below, and in the distance, he could see the ocean where he had been earlier that day. Opposite the window, the door to Farlog and Croij's quarters was ajar.

Oracus knocked, and then entered a room like nothing he had seen before. On the left half of the room, hundreds of contraptions covered shelves, tables and the floor. There were jars, bowls and flasks all hissing and giving off steam a hundred different colours, there were metal instruments that whirred and whizzed and seemed to spin of their own accord, there were clay pots full of liquids and powders, and there were tubs full of dead animal parts too. Amongst the clutter, several Sashtrams wearing aprons were stirring the contents of the jars and bowls, while others scribbled their findings on old parchment. In the midst of it all, Croij was looking particularly excited in a long white robe and goggles. He was observing a black cauldron that was spitting boiling liquid over its brim and onto the table.

In contrast, the right half of the room was calm and much more organised. There, a bookcase packed with tomes in colour order was stood behind an empty square desk with a single red quill upon it. Sat in one of three cushioned chairs beside the desk was Farlog, his wonky nose buried deep in a thick text.

A particularly loud bang from where Croij was standing was followed by something falling off a shelf and zipping across the floor. When a fat, spectacled Sashtram chased after the object, Farlog glanced up and spotted Oracus in the doorway.

"Oh, hello!" he exclaimed, jumping up much quicker than Oracus would have expected of someone his age. "I am sorry. I didn't hear you arrive over the noise. Come in, come in."

Oracus stepped forwards and shook Farlog's hand. From across the room, Croij bellowed an obscenity as the contents of his cauldron burnt a hole through the table and scorched several pages of his notes.

"Not going to plan?" Oracus muttered to Farlog.

"Worse things will happen, I assure you," he said with a knowing grin. "Would you like a drink?"

Oracus accepted the offer and took a seat. Farlog grabbed an old bottle from the bookcase and poured wine into three glasses. "Croij, come and join us," he said as he placed the bottle on the desk and passed Oracus a glass. "We have a guest."

Croij left a Sashtram to clear up his mess and joined them. He removed his goggles and wiped sweat from his brow with a handkerchief, then offered Oracus his hand.

"You mentioned this morning having a question or two for us," Farlog said, taking a long gulp of his wine.

"I have the makings of a plan to win this war," Oracus said. "But I'm keen to know some facts first."

"You sound optimistic. But facts about what?" Croij asked.

"Well, most importantly, I want to ask you what you know about the Fizorachis," Oracus asked, looking more expectantly at Farlog.

"Not a lot," Farlog said truthfully. "My books have very little information on them. Until they turned up in Fervia, nobody alive has ever encountered them."

"Do you know where they came from?"

"No idea," Farlog said with a shake of his head. "They probably have a homeland somewhere across the ocean to the north. But unless you have recently acquired a boat, I doubt that will be much help."

Oracus took a sip from his glass. The wine was smooth and sweet. "Why are they in Pharia?"

"Because they feed off life," Farlog answered. "I can only assume their homeland no longer sustains them, so they've travelled to seek life elsewhere."

"Should we expect them to spread through Pharia if they aren't stopped?"

"Certainly," Farlog stated. "Torvanon's scouts have already advised of their movement into the forest and mountains. There's plenty of life in Pharia, but who knows how quickly they will consume it all."

"Any idea how we can stop them?"

"None at all," Farlog said despairingly. "They're too quick and fierce for a simple soldier, and they drain a Rider's powers. They seem invincible."

"And there's nothing you know of that weakens them?" Oracus pressed.

"I'm afraid not," Farlog finished.

Oracus looked into the old man's eyes and felt an anxious excitement build within him. "Have you heard of the Emerald Pairing?" he asked.

Farlog put down his glass and walked over to the bookcase. "A myth, as I understand," he said. He pulled a book free and flicked through its pages. "Ah, yes. It says here that the Emerald Pairing is a mythical connection between two gemstones that grants the beholder extraordinary power."

"Does it say what that power is?" Oracus questioned.

"No, but I have read in the past a claim that the legendary King Xarmoud once owned both emeralds."

"Whoever claimed that was right," Oracus said. "Do you remember me telling you in Tallarin that I've had visions of King Xarmoud?"

"I do," Croij said. And Farlog nodded too.

"Well I dreamt once of the moment he vanquished the Fizorachis at the end of the Noble War," Oracus explained. "And I also dreamt of him donning the Emerald Pairing ready for battle."

Farlog looked thoughtful. "What do *you* think the Emerald Pairing's power is?"

Oracus pulled his sword from his belt and took the necklace from around his neck. He placed them both on the floor for the brothers to see. "I think it allows Riders to use their powers even when the Fizorachis are near," he said. "And I have both parts here."

The look of astonishment on Farlog and Croij's faces was what Oracus had been expecting. As the emeralds glowed beside each other, even the Sashtrams were anxious to have a look.

"I was so sure this was just a myth," Farlog said. "Where did you find them?"

"The sword was my father's. I assume it's been handed down father to son over centuries. I've had visions of King Xarmoud, so I suspect I'm of his blood." Oracus took another sip of his wine. "The necklace I found in the forest. The emerald in the sword guided me to it."

Farlog looked enraptured. "No wonder you spoke of rescuing Gravaz with such little concern this morning," he said. "I should warn you, however, that even with your powers, fighting the Fizorachis is likely to end badly."

"I'm not that foolish," Oracus said. "I'll try to get in and out of there without them noticing."

"I suspect it will not be so easy. You're forgetting that they feed off life. They will sense you the moment you are near."

"I've never once thought it would be easy, Farlog. But I'm confident I can do it," Oracus answered determinedly.

"And if you rescue Gravaz then you'll take him to the Ulatoris in the Black Forest?" Croij asked. "And they will rescue the prisoners from Malum?"

"I don't know," Oracus said uncertainly. "But I have to try."

"You're risking your life for a maybe?"

"I'm risking my life because those prisoners need freeing. And if the Ulatoris are willing to go to Malum, then hopefully they'll fight Jowra with us too."

"Now that would be helpful," Farlog agreed.

"You asked me in the meeting this morning where the prisoners would go once the Ulatoris freed them," Oracus said, looking at Croij. "What if they joined forces with the Ulatoris, then marched further north together and attacked Melzor from the south?"

"You're thinking of attacking Melzor?" Croij asked.

"Isn't the point of all this to kill Jowra?" Oracus said. "How else are we going to do that? If the Ulatoris attack from the south and Afarra attacks from the north, it'll force Jowra to split what's left of his army."

Farlog frowned. "Let's say Torvanon agrees to send an army to Melzor *and* you somehow convince the Ulatoris to do the same. How are we going to synchronise the two attacks?"

"This is where I need Croij's help," Oracus said. "Is there a device you can invent that would allow me to communicate with Afarra while I'm gone?"

Oracus's entire plan hinged on Croij's answer. He expected the brother to laugh at him and say its impossible. But instead, he got up and began rustling through the sheets of parchment that were scattered over his workstation. "Where is it?" he muttered to himself repeatedly. "I know it's here somewhere. Aha!" He pulled a small package from under the bubbling cauldron and walked back over to his seat.

Oracus watched keenly as Croij unwrapped the package and pulled out two square mirrors, each about the size of his hands. "What are they?" he asked.

"I made these before Tallarin was conquered as a way of Tallarin and Afarra communicating without sending messengers," Croij explained. He passed one of the mirrors to Oracus. "They're opposing mirrors. You touch your finger to the glass and you'll be able to see and speak to whoever has the other half of the pair."

Oracus looked down at the mirror and saw his own green eyes looking back at him. He carefully pressed his forefinger to the glass and it rippled like he'd dropped a stone in water. When the surface fell still again, his face had been replaced with Croij's. He gasped in shock.

"Quite the invention, right?" Croij said proudly.

"They're perfect!" Oracus exclaimed. "They're exactly what we need."

"They will work at any distance."

Oracus smiled broadly. "I think this is the final piece to my plan. May I keep this half?"

"Of course," Croij said. "Does that mean you're going to leave soon?"

"I need to talk to Torvanon first. When he's happy, I'll set off right away." Oracus stood up and drank the last of his wine. He placed his glass on the desk and tucked the mirror safely inside his shirt. "Thank you both for your help."

"Our pleasure," the brothers said together.

Oracus made for the door, but then turned back. "Before I go, can I ask you one last question?"

"Ask away," Farlog urged.

"I've been having a lot of visions of Jowra and I'm struggling to control them. Is there anything I can do to make them stop?"

"And why would you want them stop?" Farlog enquired.

"I'm worried he might realise I'm spying on him," Oracus said. "What if he uses it against me?"

"I'd be very surprised if he knew what you could do," Farlog said. "Even Jowra with his many powers can't use his mind in such a way."

"How do you know?" Oracus asked.

"Visioning is a gift you've inherited from your father's ancestors, not Jowra's. It is my understanding King Xarmoud was quite excellent at Visioning, which goes a long way in explaining why you can do it." Farlog poured himself another glass of wine as he spoke. "You should cherish these visions, Oracus. They allow you to see Jowra's plans and use them against him. It's a huge advantage for us."

"But I feel his emotions when I have these visions too. Sometimes I even think I *am* him."

"Regrettably, some gifts have their weaknesses," Farlog confessed. "That is something you'll have to learn to control."

Oracus didn't know what he'd expected Farlog to say, but the answer left him frustrated. Every time he dreamt of Jowra, he tried to control the feelings, but never with any success. And such closeness to Jowra was torturous.

"One final thing," Oracus said. And when Farlog gave him an encouraging nod, he continued. "Do you know all Jowra's powers?"

"Unfortunately, that is something only Jowra knows," Farlog said earnestly. "An advantage that he holds over us I think."

"I thought as much," Oracus replied with disappointment. He walked through the doorway and out into the corridor where the lamps had been lit. There was a sudden finality to his plan now, and with it, a sense of anxiety. He and Bandor would soon be leaving Afarra for a second time, and leaving his friends once again. It was a difficult decision to make – especially now he'd discovered happiness again – but it was also a decision he was sure would sway the outcome of the war in the rebellion's favour.

TWENTY-FIVE

Multi-Powered

Thankfully, Torvanon agreed to Oracus's plan with little argument. Although it would rely upon a considerable amount of good fortune for Oracus to succeed at every step, Torvanon was all for it if it meant another army would attack Melzor from the south. The greater the force, the higher the chance of Jowra's demise, and the fewer casualties his army would endure should they be victorious. His only concern had been the coordination of the two attacks, but with Croij's opposing mirrors, that wasn't to be a problem.

So Oracus stood facing Garrin under the shadow of the palace with his sword raised in readiness. It was to be their final time sparring before Oracus left for Fervia. They both wore the green armour of Afarra, and they were to fight with their powers and Lavorians, just as they would in battle.

"I can't believe you're going so soon," Garrin said unhappily. "Life was just getting back to how it was in Thessley."

Oracus disagreed. "Life will never be like it was in Thessley unless we win this war. And for that, I need to leave."

"I should be coming with you," Garrin claimed. "I could help you fight the Fizorachis."

"I won't be fighting them, I'll be avoiding them," Oracus said. "You need to be here assisting Torvanon."

"Still, it would help having a second Rider with you."

Oracus rolled his eyes. "Come on, let's just fight!"

Garrin grunted and scuffed the sole of his boot on the gravel.

"Bandor, are you ready for this?" Oracus said.

Bandor roared, and Oracus launched himself at Garrin, who lifted his sword to block the attack. Their blades came together and Oracus's senses heightened as Bandor entered his mind. Over the grinding of metal, he could hear Garrin's slow breathing and the clamour of other soldiers sparring nearby. He could smell the sweet flowers in the adjacent meadow too, and the beads of sweat that were already glistening on Garrin's forehead.

When Oracus pushed Garrin away, he took a moment to steady himself. Then he attempted a second strike, but Garrin was equal to that too.

"You aren't going to beat me that easy, Vassath Rider," Garrin provoked.

The loose ground around them started to shake and rise, and a small tornado grew at their feet. Oracus found himself scanning the city with his mind, searching for any power he could defend himself with. He could feel Torvanon, Kivali and Dyma nearby, but nothing would help him against rocks and stones.

The tornado built to a cyclone that had the soldiers nearby running for cover. Oracus covered his face with his hands as sand scratched his skin and stones bounced off his armour. He would be forced to surrender soon, because he was helplessly overpowered.

"Use Dyma's shield!" Bandor shouted.

Oracus quickly did as his Lavorian suggested and a transparent red orb appeared, encasing both Oracus and Garrin and separating them from the cyclone outside. Now safe from the rocks, Oracus dropped his hands and thrust his sword at Garrin. Garrin blocked cleverly, but Oracus came back with several more strikes that drew his friend's concentration away from his power. The stones fell from the sky and clanged noisily on the shield, and Oracus felt stronger than ever as Bandor sucked all the emotion from his mind.

"Try to use more than one power," his Lavorian encouraged.

Oracus was sure he could use two powers at once; he'd just never had the chance before. So with Dyma's power still intact, he focused on Kivali's mind too. Then just as Garrin was about to strike his ribs with his blade, Oracus vanished and reappeared at Garrin's shoulder. Garrin's blade carved air, and Oracus rested his own blade against his friend's neck. For only a brief moment, Dyma's shield had flickered.

"How did you do that?" Garrin bellowed in frustration. "That's not fair!"

"I'm a Vassath Rider," Oracus joked. "And it turns out beating you is quite easy!"

With little warning, Garrin swung his sword downwards and cut Oracus's leg between the joint of his armour. Dyma's shield crumbled as Oracus lost focus and Garrin escaped his clutches. As the cyclone converged on him once again, he dropped to his knees with a yell of pain.

"Bandor, I need your help!" he begged.

The pain in his leg ceased as he felt his Lavorian delve deeper into his mind than he ever had before.

"Use Garrin's power to stop the storm," Bandor urged.

Oracus closed his eyes and obliged. The wind suddenly stopped wailing and the force of the billowing gusts died down. When Oracus snapped his eyes open, the sight made his jaw drop. Every stone and grain of sand had become motionless and hung in the air like gravity had been switched off. All around, the dust lingered, and the silence it held was serene.

From somewhere nearby, Bandor approached, and through the dust he eventually emerged. *"You're getting stronger, Rider,"* he said. *"Get on and we'll ride together."*

As Oracus climbed onto Bandor's back, some of the stones in the air wobbled defiantly, like Garrin was fighting back. But with Bandor aiding him, Oracus was in control. Blood trickled down his leg, and the scratches on his face oozed, yet he felt the pain no longer. And as Bandor ran from the sparring area, he released his power and the cyclone raged once again behind them.

The glory of freedom coursed through Oracus as Bandor reached the meadow. They were in the sun now, and the light glistened in Bandor's armour. The scent of long grass and wildflowers pervaded the air, and the green pines in the woodland beyond it carried their own distinct aroma.

As Bandor bounded through the grass, his control over Oracus's emotions slipped momentarily and his delight was carried into his Rider's mind. For a few seconds, Oracus could feel his Lavorian's love for him, and he cherished it with all his heart. At that time, nothing else mattered – not Jowra, not the war, not the Fizorachis – because they were together. And their trust for each other was like nothing Oracus had ever felt. He knew Bandor would stay by his side, no matter what was to happen.

A screech from above snatched the feelings away from Oracus too soon. Aquila and Garrin had taken flight and were gliding overhead, bearing down on them. Bandor arced his run and headed back towards the palace, where they could escape between the nearby buildings. But the gusts of wind from Aquila's wings almost unseated Oracus, and he knew they'd never make it.

"Faster, Bandor," he ordered.

"I can't!" Bandor shouted in reply.

Oracus desperately fixed his mind on Dyma's power and surrounded them with her shield once again. But Aquila's talons pierced it and left Oracus vulnerable once more.

"I've got you now!" Garrin cried out triumphantly as Aquila closed in.

In the moment Oracus had to retaliate, he connected to the one mind he hadn't yet used – Torvanon's. Although not as powerful as Jowra's, Torvanon's mind was still immense enough to make Oracus grimace, and it took all his concentration to control it. But control it he did. And when Aquila was about snatch him from Bandor's saddle, he held up his hand and brought her to a halt.

The Eagle looked to have hit an invisible wall she stopped so abruptly. But her momentum had been such that Garrin was thrown headlong from her back and directly into Bandor's path. Before Oracus had even considered celebrating, Garrin slammed into him and knocked him off Bandor and onto the harsh gravel path.

Oracus skidded to a halt and breathed heavily as he lay on his back. When he sat up, he looked over at Garrin and they both started laughing.

"That was incredible!" Oracus said.

"It really was," Garrin agreed. "The way you used all those powers was really impressive!"

"And I still couldn't beat you," Oracus said, inspired by the tenacity his friend had shown. "Is Aquila alright?"

"She's fine," he replied, looking to where she had fallen.

From across the meadow, Oracus could see her taking to the sky again. In a few seconds, she was gliding over the grass to join them.

"You know you can't come with me to Fervia, don't you?" Oracus said, becoming more serious. After experiencing such joy, the task ahead was finally beginning to dawn on him. There was so much danger to come, it was possible they wouldn't see each other again once Oracus left.

Garrin nodded. "I'm needed here, I know," he said. "It doesn't make it any easier though."

"No," Oracus agreed. "But soon the war will be over and we'll be fighting like this every morning."

"Every morning?" Garrin said with a laugh. "After killing Jowra, we'd end up killing each other."

"We nearly did that once or twice as children too," Oracus said.

"Those are memories I'll never forget," Garrin said happily.

Oracus stood up himself and hit his friend playfully on the shoulder. "Come on, let's get some breakfast," he said. "We're beginning to sound like sentimental old men here."

They both gave themselves a final wipe down and sheathed their swords. Then they headed to the palace to join the morning feast.

TWENTY-SIX

Aspiring Associates

It was the evening before Oracus and Bandor were due to leave for Fervia and a cool dusk had enveloped Afarra. Far into the distance, above the furthest reaches of the Raspian Forest, flickers of lightning lit up the sky.

A delicate breeze made Oracus shiver. It felt cold for a change, a sure sign that Pharia was changing. Oracus was in the cemetery, visiting his father's grave for what may have been the final time. As golden leaves rolled by on the wind, he found comfort in knowing he might soon be reunited with him.

"It's a blessing you didn't have to see any of this, father," he whispered to the grave. "You're far safer wherever you are."

For a moment, Oracus expected his father's voice to respond to him, but the sound of crisp leaves and creaking trees went unchallenged.

"I would give anything right now to feel your arm around my shoulder one last time," he said. "You would tell me all the words I needed to hear. You knew how to make me feel brave whenever I was scared."

For Oracus *was* scared. When Bandor wasn't controlling his emotions, he was utterly terrified. But it wasn't death that brought him fear; it was far more complicated than that. It was arriving in Valaroth without Gravaz. It was losing the war to Jowra. It was being conquered by the Fizorachis. It was leaving his friends behind to deal with the catastrophe if he died. In essence, it was failure. And an inability to carry out what he'd promised.

"I need you to watch over me, father. Don't let me make a mistake." Oracus felt a lump forming in his throat, but he forced the feeling away. Now wasn't the time for weakness.

Another current of cold air swept through the cemetery and a gentle hand grasped Oracus's arm, making him jump. It was Kivali, and she looked resplendent in a blue dress that reminded Oracus of the time they'd kissed in Tallarin. He felt his chest tighten, and his mouth suddenly felt very dry.

"Hi," he managed to say.

"Hi," she replied. "Sorry I scared you. I wanted to make sure you were alright."

Her forget-me-not eyes were wide and alert, and her brown hair black in the darkness. She was feeling the cold, for her bare arms were covered in gooseflesh and her knuckles were a shade of blue.

"You've been avoiding me," she said.

"I haven't," Oracus lied.

"Have I really upset you *that* much?" she asked. "You won't even let me apologise properly."

"I didn't see the point," Oracus said. "I knew I wouldn't be here for long so it would have been a waste of time."

"We could have tried to make the most of it."

Oracus glared at her. "I spent a whole year praying you were still alive. Then when I arrived here, you were the first person I wanted to see. But I found out you'd accused me of working with the man who killed my father!"

"And I was wrong to do that," she said. "I'm sorry, alright. What else can I say?"

Oracus shook his head and turned away from her. "I was avoiding you because I didn't want this conversation. I'm glad you're alive, and I appreciate your apology, but I'm leaving tomorrow so it's all a little too late."

Kivali stepped closer to him and wrapped her arms around his midriff. The feel of her touch made him tense. "I really am sorry for what I said. I never actually thought you'd work for him, I was just upset and confused."

"It's fine," Oracus said. He allowed his muscles to loosen and hugged her back.

"But I'll have plenty of time to make up for it over the next few weeks," she said. "What I really came here for was to tell you I'm coming with you."

Oracus pushed her away. "You're not! It's too dangerous."

"I've already agreed it with Torvanon," she said.

"Then *un-agree* it with him."

"Oracus, you have no choice. Farlog and Croij told me about the Emerald Pairing and what it does."

"I'll be able to use my powers around the Fizorachis, yes," he said.

"But whose power will you copy if you're there alone?" she stated. "Think about it. You'll need me there so you can teleport in and out quickly."

Her point was a valid one, and Oracus found it difficult to argue otherwise.

"And Dyma's coming too," Kivali added. "Should you need to protect yourself, you can use her shields."

"No, this is crazy. Torvanon needs you both here. What if Jowra attacks?"

"Torvanon is more powerful than the rest of us put together. And he has Garrin here with him," Kivali answered. "If Jowra came here then it would be more dangerous than if I were in Fervia. At least if I'm with you then you can keep me safe."

And those were the words that convinced Oracus to agree. The frustration that had been building inside him suddenly eased, and he felt a desire for Kivali that had been missing since his return to Afarra. "Fine," he said. "But it won't just be a trip to Fervia. The Black Forest will be our destination after that."

"I've already packed warm clothes," Kivali answered. She shivered as a gust of wind ruffled her dress. "Talking of warm clothes, I'm really cold. Can we go inside?"

Oracus took one last doleful look at his father's grave. "Sure," he said.

Kivali took his hand, and then the cemetery was gone. In an instant, he was out of the darkness and into Kivali's quarters in the palace. The room was empty besides the bed and a dark green rug on the floor, and it was lit by several bright oil-lamps. The walls were decorated in green and gold patterns, and there was a door that Oracus suspected Kivali rarely used.

"It's much warmer in here," Kivali said with a sigh. She kicked off her shoes and sat on the bed.

Oracus felt a rush of excitement, for he'd noticed that Onca was absent. She would usually be in Kivali's quarters, he thought, so why wasn't she now? Kivali obviously wanted to spend time with him alone.

But unfortunately, they weren't alone. There was someone in the room waiting for them.

"'ello, Mr Oracus," a quiet voice uttered.

Kivali screamed, and embarrassingly, so did Oracus.

From the corner, a mousy boy with freckles stepped forward. He was wearing clothes much too large for him.

"What are you doing in here, Nivin?" Oracus shouted in alarm.

Nivin swayed guiltily on the spot. "I came ter speak ter yer before yer leave ter'morrow," he said.

Oracus put his hands on his knees and breathed deeply. "How did you know I was going to be in this room?"

Nivin shrugged his shoulders; the same shrug he'd offered Oracus several times on their last encounter.

"And how did you know I was leaving tomorrow?"

"Jus' did," the boy replied simply.

Kivali looked from Oracus to Nivin, and then back at Oracus. "Who is he?" she asked.

"He's called Nivin. He's Morpac's son."

"Morpac from Tallarin?" Kivali said. "Is he here in Afarra?"

Oracus looked sadly at Nivin. "No, he was killed in Tallarin. Nivin is here alone."

"Oh, I'm so sorry," Kivali said. She got up and walked over to the boy.

"Tha's alrigh', Ma'am. It weren't yer fault."

When Kivali pulled him into a hug, Nivin looked particularly pleased with himself.

"How did you get in here?" Oracus asked him next.

"Through the door, Sir," Nivin said.

"But the door was locked," Kivali contended.

"I unlocked it," Nivin answered with a rueful smile. He pulled the same length of wire out his shirt that he had planned to use on Oracus's cell door in the prison.

Kivali held him at arm's length and looked at him sternly. "The guards would likely have killed you if they'd caught you picking the lock."

"I don't get caugh', Ma'am," he said. "Besides, it were worth the risk. I wanna know if I can travel ter Fervia with both o' yer?"

"How do you know we're going to Fervia together?" Kivali asked. "We've only just discussed it!"

Oracus waved his hand dismissively. "You're wasting your breath. He knows everything but never admits how." He turned to Nivin. "I'm sorry but you can't come with us."

"Please, please, please, Mr Oracus. Yer won' even know am there!" he argued.

"You're just a boy. It's far too dangerous."

"Am not a boy no more, Sir. Me parents are dead, jus' like yours, so I wanna fight."

The bluntness of Nivin's argument surprised Oracus. His wide eyes were still innocent, but determined now too. Oracus crouched down and looked him in the face. "I know you want to help," he said. "But I'd prefer you to stay here where it's safe."

"Am not scared o' dyin'," Nivin claimed.

"I didn't say you were. I think you're really brave," Oracus said. "But I already regret not saving my mother and father's lives. I don't need *your* death on my conscience too."

Nivin bowed his head wistfully and shuffled over to the door. "I understand," he said sadly. "I guess al jus' see yer when ye'r back then."

Oracus felt bad as the boy closed the door behind him, but guilt was never going to make him change his mind. Nivin was probably waiting outside with his ear pressed against the keyhole, hoping Oracus would call him back.

Kivali looked at Oracus, puzzled. "Is this what it's come to?" she asked. "Young boys want to take the place of their dead fathers on the battlefield?"

"Apparently so," Oracus replied.

Kivali put her arms around him again. But it wasn't the hug of passion he had expected when they first teleported to her bedroom, it was a hug of distress.

"The sooner we kill Jowra, the sooner children like Nivin can live normal lives again," he said. "Come tomorrow, we'll have started on a journey to put right some of the wrongs he's created."

"I hope so," Kivali said. "Because what that boy has been through is heart-breaking."

Twenty-Seven

Unfathomable Secret

Dawn arrived with cloudy skies and fine rain the next morning. And far to the east, thunder growled menacingly from above the Raspian Forest.

Oracus had donned his green leather armour in preparation for the trip to Fervia. His sword and dagger were attached to his belt too, his bow and quiver strapped tightly over his shoulder, and the emerald necklace tied around his neck. Once he'd filled his pack, he fastened the saddle to Bandor's back and walked to the city gate.

When Oracus previously left Afarra, he had been ignorant to the dangers he was likely to face. He'd had no concerns about not seeing Garrin again, nor not being able to visit his father's grave. But this time was different, he was well aware now of the perils awaiting him out there. It was quite possible this would be the last time he saw his friend or the cemetery. Garrin must have felt the same apprehension because they clasped each other in a longer-than-usual embrace.

"Keep that mirror near to you," Oracus ordered. "We'll talk regularly."

"If you get spotted in Fervia then just get out of there," Garrin advised. "Don't risk getting caught for Gravaz."

"I won't," Oracus assured. He ran his fingers over the necklace, the emerald was resting against the chest-piece of his armour. "I'll have my powers too though remember. I'll be able to defend myself if I need to."

Garrin looked worriedly at Oracus as they broke apart. "Stay safe," he said. "Keep me informed of everything that happens when you're gone."

The portcullis began to clang upwards while the drawbridge lowered to the grassy bank on the far side of the moat. Oracus looked out over the vast and empty grassland and saw nothing but a herd of deer grazing in the shadow of the forest in the distance.

Kivali and Dyma appeared at Oracus's shoulder with Onca and Huadlan. With their blue armour, they both carried with them a homage to Tallarin. Onca, being a Jaguar, was more slender than Bandor, despite being as tall. And Huadlan the Orangutan was slightly taller than Oracus when leaning forwards on his fists.

"Time to go, Oracus," Kivali said when Torvanon arrived to see them leave.

Oracus pulled himself onto Bandor's back and sat back in the saddle. He patted the Lion's side affectionately and sprinkled his mind with courage. Kivali jumped into Onca's saddle, whilst Dyma stepped into the stirrups of a strange harness wrapped around Huadlan's shoulders. When she wrapped her arms around his neck, he could carry her comfortably on his back.

"See you both soon," Oracus said, looking down at Garrin and Torvanon. He nodded encouragingly at Kivali, and they proceeded out the city.

The rain seemed to fall harder the moment they crossed the moat. With his hair already sticking to his face, Oracus urged Bandor towards the shelter of the forest. The three Lavorians stepped up their pace, and Oracus was able to appreciate the open space for a change. He gripped Bandor tight with his thighs, raised his arms in the air, and whooped happily. It was few minutes of freedom to enjoy before the trees were upon them and they would have to battle their way through the undergrowth.

The eerie quiet and lack of light were what Oracus noticed most when the forest first surrounded him. When he had hunted there as a teen, and even when he had travelled through there a few weeks ago, it had been full of birdsong and animal-chatter, and slithers of sunlight breaking through the canopy. Now, there was only the purr of rainwater on the leaves above, and the light was barely enough for Human eyes to see.

"We should aim to reach Fervia by nightfall," Oracus proposed. "The sooner we get there, the less the Fizorachis will have spread."

Huadlan swung and jumped through the branches overhead while Bandor and Onca splashed through puddles that had formed on the wet forest floor. Barely ten minutes had passed by and Oracus was already covered in scratches from hanging vines and thorny bushes. He wondered briefly if Artus Mor grew in the Raspian Forest so he could repair his wounds, but then something resembling a child ran across their path and took them all by surprise. Bandor skidded to a halt to avoid the child, and Oracus was thrown from his back. He hit a tree hard, and then landed face down in the mud.

It took a few seconds for Oracus to realise what had happened. He groaned as he pushed himself up, for every part of his body hurt.

"Are you okay?" Kivali asked as she jumped off Onca's back to help Oracus to his feet. "What was that?"

"I don't know," Oracus answered. "It looked like a child, but it was probably a deer or something."

"No, it was a child!" Bandor said. The Lion had chased the creature into the trees and come back out with a young, freckly boy in his jaws.

"Am so sorry, Mr Oracus. Please don' let yer Lion eat me!"

"You've got to be joking!" Oracus exclaimed. "Nivin? What are you doing here?"

Bandor spat Nivin onto the floor. "I wan'ed ter travel with yer, Mr Oracus," the boy said sheepishly.

"How did you get out the city?" Oracus demanded.

"Through the gate," Nivin said vaguely.

"Without any guards seeing you?"

"I guess so."

Oracus stomped over to Nivin and grabbed him by the collar of his baggy shirt. "How do you keep finding me like this? What powers do you have?"

Nivin's lip quivered and he started to cry, so Oracus let him go.

"You can do things I've never seen before," Oracus said. "This forest is huge. How did you know we'd pass through this exact place?"

"I don' know," he stammered innocently. "I jus' did."

"And why find me this far into the forest? Why not just meet me before we left?"

"'cause back there yer'd 'ave said no again," Nivin explained dejectedly. "But now yer'll 'ave ter take me with yer!"

"I won't. You have to go home," Oracus forced, pointing in the direction they'd come. "I've already told you it's too dangerous."

"It's not me 'ome, Mr Oracus. I 'ave nowhere ter call 'ome anymore. I answer ter nobody an' I'm free ter come with yer if I wanna."

"We're going to a place full of creatures who only want to hurt us. They won't care that you're young, they will kill you anyway."

"It's me own choice!" Nivin said defiantly. "If yer aren' gonna let me travel with yer then al jus' meet yer there."

"We intend to arrive by evening. There's no way you'd get there by then."

"Would yer care ter bet on tha'?" Nivin said.

The boy smiled furtively and Oracus frowned. The secret Nivin was keeping was a mystery he just couldn't solve.

"Ye'r gonna try an' free a prisoner," Nivin said. "Oo der yer know tha's be'er than me at sneakin' inter places tha' shouldn' be sneaked inter?"

Oracus couldn't hold back a laugh. "Fine!" he said. "You can come with us. But you will not be doing any *sneaking*."

Nivin jumped up and down gleefully. "Thank yer, Mr Oracus. Thank yer so much!" He hugged Oracus around his waist, then skipped over to Bandor and tried to pat his head. When he realised he couldn't reach, he settled for stroking the Lion's foreleg instead.

"He's persistent, that's for sure," Kivali said.

"I know," Oracus replied. "Have you ever met anyone like him?"

Kivali shook her head, but Dyma spoke up instead. "I have. There was a group of them in Tallarin."

"Did you know any of them personally?" Oracus asked.

"No. I spent most of my time in the palace and they used to travel outside the city," Dyma said.

Oracus remembered saving Nivin's father from Grevlors and Lisors in the mountains outside Tallarin. "Do you know how many others there are?" he asked.

Dyma lowered her voice so Nivin couldn't hear. "None alive now, I suspect. They all lived near the fortress and didn't leave their homes when Jowra's army arrived. They would all have been killed."

Oracus frowned and looked over at the poor boy, who was now trying to clamber up Bandor's side. "Come on," he said to everyone. "We need to get moving again." He walked over to Nivin and gave him a helpful push. When he was astride Bandor's back, Oracus jumped into the saddle behind him.

"We're awfully high!" Nivin exclaimed.

Oracus ruffled his hair. "Are you comfortable?"

"I think so."

"Good. Now make sure you hold on tight!"

TWENTY-EIGHT

Fervia's New Inhabitants

Until late afternoon they raced through the forest without stopping. The rain was unrelenting and Oracus's feet were soon damp and cold. His wet hair itched his forehead and his body ached from the constant riding. He thought the conditions would eventually wear Nivin down, but the boy talked incessantly. By the time evening came, both he and Bandor had a throbbing headache.

When darkness came, it was difficult to tell whether it was because of time or because the black storm was swirling overhead. They had almost reached their destination on the most eastern part of the forest, and the fierce flashes of lightning lit up their path every few seconds. The bellows of thunder that followed were deafening, and the winds howled and gave Oracus shivers.

"We must be close now. This is how the storm was on the battlefield when we fled," Kivali shouted so everyone could hear her. "We need to be careful."

A matter of seconds later, Dyma ordered everyone to stop. "Have you seen the leaves?" she said, holding up a hand.

Oracus dismounted Bandor and studied the bushes around him. The leaves were black and withered. "They must be nearby," he said. "Can either of you use your powers?"

They both focused for a moment and then looked worried. "No."

Oracus became anxious himself, but when he attempted his power, Dyma's red shield encased them all, and the two gems on his necklace and sword glowed and vibrated. "At least we know the Emerald Pairing works," he said, relieved. He made the shield vanish and then trudged through the mud, sniffing the air with Bandor's senses. "Dyma, I want you and Huadlan to take Nivin to the edge of the forest and wait there. Stay out of danger, but close enough to Fervia that I can use your power should I need it. Kivali and I will find you when we've rescued Gravaz."

"I want to come with you," Nivin argued.

"Absolutely not. Do what I ask and go with Dyma."

Nivin looked disappointed, but he allowed Dyma to lead him away.

When they were out of sight, Oracus turned to the others. "Farlog told me the Fizorachis will be able to sense any life that comes their way," he explained. He looked at Bandor and Onca. "As we proceed, I need you two to sense them before they sense us."

Oracus mounted Bandor again and the Lion advanced tentatively. It sounded like the thunder had mellowed now, and every snapping twig made him rub the hilt of his sword warily.

In no time at all, Bandor's whiskers were twitching. *"There's a group of them to the right of us,"* he uttered.

"Let's keep to the left then," Oracus advised. *"I don't want to face any before we have to."*

They arced to the left and continued. Oracus turned to Kivali and Onca and pressed his finger to his lips, urging them to keep quiet. He faced forwards again and stared into the void between the trees. Beneath him, Bandor prowled through the undergrowth in silence, and Oracus was reminded of the cub that had killed a mouse in his father's barn. The fate of that mouse was why Oracus had called his Lavorian Bandor; he'd read about a Bandor in one of his childhood books, *The Beasts of Legend* – *'The Bandor is the predator of all predators, so if you are unfortunate enough to encounter it, then may you rest in peace'* – the thought gave Oracus a surge of courage.

Several minutes passed by before Bandor spoke again. *"There's another one ahead,"* he said.

"Is it alone?" Oracus asked.

"Yes."

"Okay. I want to draw this one to us and kill it. That way we'll know what we're up against," Oracus said. He held up his hand to stop Kivali and Onca. "I'll be back in a second," he mouthed.

He slid quietly off Bandor's back and moved lightly between the trees. Bandor forced his senses upon Oracus and the darkness was illuminated for him, yet the fear of the unknown remained wholesome.

And then he saw it; a creature as pale as an Eevek but taller than an Ulatori. It was a harrowing beast with a hairless white head and purple veins riddling its skin. Where two eyes and a mouth should have been in its face, there were three cavernous black holes instead, as if its features had been gouged out with a spoon. In driving rain that drenched Oracus, the Fizorachi was totally dry, like it repelled the water somehow. It wore shiny black armour and held a jagged sword in its pearl-white hand. Unsurprisingly, it looked exactly as the Fizorachis had done in Oracus's dream of King Xarmoud.

The moment the Fizorachi had come into view, Oracus hid behind a tree. But the Fizorachi had sensed him already, and when Oracus peered around the tree, it faced him and cocked its head.

Oracus was suddenly petrified, and regretted ever leaving Afarra. Not since the era of King Xarmoud had anyone ever faced a Fizorachi, and Oracus didn't know what to expect when he challenged it.

"Calm down," Bandor said. *"Wait for it to come to you."*

Oracus obeyed his Lavorian and silently urged the Fizorachi to advance, which it eventually did. As it came for him, it glided like it was skating across a frozen pond; there was not a snapped twig or rustled leaf to be heard. But when it was only a few feet from him, Oracus could hear its rattling breath and smell its putrid essence.

There was no time left for him to act. Courageously, he leapt at the Fizorachi from behind the tree and slashed his sword through its pale neck. For a second, the Fizorachi remained motionless; its wide mouth and empty eye-sockets were stretched open in a way that resembled surprise, but then its milky skin and bones crumbled to dust, and its armour dropped to the floor.

Oracus would have whooped in celebration had he not feared attracting more Fizorachis. Instead, he satisfied himself with a triumphant grin and urged Bandor to proceed. *"It's dead, come on,"* he said.

No more enemies were encountered from then until the

edge of the forest. When they finally stepped out of the trees, the view over Fervia was quite terrifying. They were truly at the centre of the storm now, and the rods of lightning struck the ground within Fervia's walls. The buildings inside the city had been fortified with an alien substance of some kind, spiky and black, and Oracus could see it pulsating like a heartbeat.

Oracus looked at Kivali and saw she was wide-eyed. "How are you feeling?" he asked.

"I'm trying to comprehend what I'm seeing," she answered.

Oracus could see there were no guards around the perimeter of the city, but thousands of them manned the grounds inside.

"Gravaz is in the prison where I was held," Oracus said to the others. "Bandor, Onca, you should stay here. You'll only attract attention to us. Kivali and I will teleport into the prison and search for Gravaz. When we find him, we'll teleport back here."

Oracus grabbed Kivali's hand and held her close; it was a moment of pleasure within a world of sheer madness. Then the Lavorians, the forest, and the storm became a blur before they teleported to a stairwell inside the stone prison.

It was exceptionally dark in there, and oddly quiet too. The storm outside had been almost silenced by the denseness of the fortified black walls. The staircase Oracus and Kivali would have to climb spiralled high above them, to a floor where Oracus knew the cells were. It wasn't guarded, but Oracus gestured for Kivali to remain quiet anyway.

They kept a firm grip of each other as they ascended. Oracus could feel his heart thumping in his chest he was so scared, and he wished his footsteps wouldn't echo so loudly.

"We're at the top of the stairs, Bandor," Oracus found himself relaying when they reached a small landing. *"Make sure you stay in my mind."*

They were faced now with a bolted metal door and no view of the room ahead. Oracus knew it to be a narrow corridor with little room to move from side to side. He cursed under his breath. "We're going to have to teleport through," he whispered.

"What if there are Fizorachis on the other side?" Kivali murmured in response.

"Get your sword ready, just in case."

They both quietly unsheathed their weapons and Kivali pressed herself against Oracus's chest again. He took a deep breath, then teleported beyond.

It was a relief to find the corridor empty when their feet hit the floor. It was exactly as Oracus remembered, with little to see but the damp stone walls and several sealed cell doors on either side. After a dozen cells, the corridor turned a corner.

"This is it. This is where I was imprisoned," Oracus said faintly. "Hopefully Gravaz is in one of these."

Each door was solid steel, with a small slot in the centre that had once allowed the Grevlor guards to observe their prisoners. Oracus moved to the closest cell to check if Gravaz was held within, but before he could look, a familiar voice from the end of the corridor made his heart sink.

"Mr Oracus, I've found 'im. I've found Gravaz!"

Nivin was stood facing them and looking delighted with himself, his big brown eyes full of triumph.

"Be quiet!" Oracus mouthed.

"'e's over 'ere! Come an' see!"

"They'll hear you!" Oracus hissed.

But it was too late. From behind Nivin, a Fizorachi had appeared; a giant compared to its victim. Oracus watched helplessly as the Fizorachi grabbed the boy and thrust its sword through his torso from back to front.

Shock and pain replaced joy as Nivin felt the blade pierce him. In the seconds that followed, Oracus had teleported to Nivin's side and turned the Fizorachi to dust with his own sword. But the damage was already done.

Nivin's body fell to the floor and blood began to pool around him. Suddenly, Oracus was overwhelmed with memories of his mother – he saw her fall to his own arrow and bleed out on the white marble. He heard Quent's voice goading him. Then there was an explosion, the ocean and darkness.

Nivin coughed weakly and brought Oracus back into himself. He was sat with the boy's body cradled in his arms. "It's going to be okay," he was saying. "We're going to get you out of here." He removed his necklace. "Kivali, take this and my sword. Teleport back to the forest with Nivin."

"I'm not leaving you here unarmed," she said forcefully.

"I need to find Gravaz," he said. "I'm not getting this far and leaving without him!"

"I can't do that."

"I just need you to do what I ask. Please. Now go!"

Her eyes pleaded with him, but it was no use. "Go," he repeated.

Kivali conceded and pulled the necklace over her head. When she grabbed his sword, she gave him one last glance, then vanished with Nivin.

Oracus was now very much alone.

TWENTY-NINE

Casualties Of War

Oracus stood for a moment and stared at the shallow puddle of blood that had been left behind. His overwhelming terror was now matched by a feeling of fury. This time though, it wasn't Jowra's fury, but his own.

Oracus forced himself to move forwards. But without his powers or a sword, he felt vulnerable. When he reached the turn in the corridor, he was faced with six more cells, and three horrifying Fizorachis that guarded them.

Oracus pressed himself against the cold wall and kept out of sight. If he was to defeat his adversaries with his bare hands, he would need to surprise them. The situation called for a plan, but with only a short dagger for a weapon, he felt helpless.

He stared at the floor for a while and wondered if the Fizorachis might just leave, but then another familiar voice called out to him, and filled him with more dread.

"Oracus," it said. "Oracus, are you there?"

Croij's opposing mirror was in his backpack and Garrin was calling to him from the other end. His timing couldn't have been worse.

"Oracus!" he shouted.

Oracus tussled frantically with the fastenings of his pack, but the Fizorachis were already coming to investigate. He could hear their breath and smell their odour from around the corner.

When they appeared, their jagged swords were drawn ready, and their ghostly faces were stretched into jubilant surprise. Oracus barely had time to react as the first Fizorachi lunged at him with its weapon. He dodged to the right, but the sword grazed his hand and he felt warm blood ooze from the wound. The second and third Fizorachis then attacked and Oracus took a blow to his ribs and a cut to his cheek. He groaned and dropped to his knees, dagger in hand but useless. The Fizorachis struck again with speed, and Oracus was forced to roll away from the attacks. But now he was surrounded, sat exposed against the wall with no means of escape.

He looked up at the gruesome faces of the Fizorachis and expected the end to come, but Garrin shouted his name from the mirror again and the voice distracted the Fizorachis. Oracus took his chance and jumped up at the one that had sliced his face. With a well-placed stab to the head, he turned the Fizorachi to dust and caught its sword on the way to the floor.

The two remaining Fizorachis let out an unworldly scream that cracked the walls and forced Oracus to cover his ears. He quickly realised the wail wasn't to incapacitate him, but to warn the rest of the city of his presence. So he fought through the sound and killed both Fizorachis with his new blade. But the alarm had already been raised, and Oracus had no choice but to wipe the blood from his face and find Gravaz as quickly as he could.

The Ulatori was in the last cell Oracus checked, sitting on the stone bed and gazing far into the distance. When Oracus threw open the door, Gravaz turned to face his rescuer, but seemed not to care.

"We have to leave," Oracus shouted at him. "Fizorachis will be swarming us in less than a minute."

The Ulatori was slighter than he'd once been, but still frighteningly large. His skin was the same dull grey as all the Ulatoris and his head bald like most Ulatori men. But Gravaz had scarring across his face and chest from where Oracus had hit him with a fireball. One of his eyes was golden yellow, but the other, which once had a patch on it, was blank and misty white.

"I thought you were dead," he said to Oracus in a deep, calm voice.

"Luckily for you, I'm not," Oracus answered frankly. He pointed his newly acquired sword at Gravaz. "Get moving."

The Ulatori was happy to obey Oracus. "Lead the way," he said without question.

Oracus returned to the corridor and headed back towards the staircase with Gravaz close on his tail. At any other time, he would have bound Gravaz's hands and frogmarched him forwards, but he was so eager to escape, he cared little for whether the Ulatori would attack him from behind. *"I've got Gravaz,"* he projected with his mind. *"But the Fizorachis know I'm here."*

"Lots of them just came from the forest and entered the city," Bandor replied. *"There are hundreds coming for you."*

"I don't know how we're going to get out, Bandor."

"Just focus on fleeing the prison. As soon as you're out, we'll be there to teleport you away."

When Oracus and Gravaz reached the metal door at the top of the stairway, a half-dozen Fizorachis came through it to meet them. Their faces were expressionless, but Oracus suspected they were less than happy with Oracus for trying to steal their prisoner. They rasped to each other as they glided forwards, and Oracus sliced two of their throats and ducked swiftly under the strike of a third. Gravaz ripped a fourth in half with his bare hands, while Oracus dispatched of the third and killed the remaining two with well-timed thrusts.

They pushed through into the landing atop the staircase and descended as more Fizorachis approached from below. Gravaz had taken a sword from the dead, and Oracus might well have been side-by-side with Sarvon the two Ulatoris looked so similar. Gravaz slayed the Fizorachis like Sarvon would too, using his strength to ruthlessly carve through them. By the time they reached the bottom, ten more Fizorachis had been turned to dust.

They charged through the door of the prison and found themselves in the centre of the churning black storm. It circled in a vortex above, and the winds knocked Oracus off his feet. From the blackened ground, he looked up and squinted through the rain at thousands of Fizorachis surrounding him and Gravaz. Unmoved by the weather, they waited like a wave of tar ready to crash down on them.

"Now would be a great time to get us out of here!" Oracus shouted at Bandor.

The Fizorachis closed in and their many white faces glared victoriously.

"Get up," Bandor ordered. *"We're almost there."*

"Almost whe–"

Before Oracus had a chance to stand, Bandor broke through the wall of Fizorachis and scattered them in all directions. Their screams of surprise pierced the roar of the cyclone and Oracus was forced to cover his ears again.

Bandor galloped closer and Oracus could see Kivali riding him, her hair whipping from side to side and the emerald necklace bouncing against her chest. Oracus grabbed Gravaz's thick wrist, and the moment Bandor reached him, the ferocity of the storm was swallowed by Kivali's power. When Oracus opened his eyes, he was sheltered by the forest, and he breathed a huge sigh of relief. There were thick trees all around him, keeping him safe, and he couldn't see the storm clouds through the canopy overhead. In the distance, heard the enraged screams of the Fizorachis they'd just escaped.

Gravaz was the first of them all to move, and he approached Oracus with the Fizorachi's sword in his hand. Oracus expected the Ulatori to try and kill him, but he simply placed the sword at Oracus's feet.

"You rescued me," he said. And he bowed his head in gratitude.

The Ulatori's respect surprised Oracus, but he didn't let it show on his face. Nor did he acknowledge it. He scratched Bandor's chin instead and turned to Kivali. "That was incredible," he said. "You saved my life again."

"It was Bandor too," she replied modestly. She passed Oracus his sword and looped the necklace over his head. "But don't ever put me in that position again. I shouldn't have left you."

The speed and exhilaration of battle had cocooned Oracus's mind, but he suddenly remembered Nivin. When he spotted the young boy on the ground, he rushed over to him.

"He's still alive, but he's really weak," Kivali said.

Nivin was pale as snow, and the wound on his stomach was gushing blood. He was lying against Onca's side, propped up on a bed of leaves with a blanket over him.

"Where's Dyma?" Oracus demanded, suddenly angry. "Her and Huadlan were supposed to be watching him."

But the scream of a woman to the south drew everyone's attention, and an answer never came. The anger Oracus was feeling quickly dissipated.

"Everybody wait here," he said. "It's safer for me with my powers."

He rushed into the trees to find the source of the scream, but now there was just the grumble of the storm and he struggled to locate it. For what must have been ten minutes, he searched frantically, until he no longer knew where he was. He scanned the trees around him, but there was nothing except bark and leaves for him to see.

"Can you hear me?" he shouted hopefully into the darkness.

A second scream came, much closer than the first, and Oracus recognised it as Dyma. He pressed on through the trees, reinvigorated, but when he came to the clearing where she was, he was flooded with fear at the scene that met him.

A Fizorachi much larger than those Oracus had faced in Fervia was standing tall and proud beside a creature twice the size of Bandor. The Fizorachi was dressed in majestic black armour with spikes covering the shoulders, and in his hand he held a sword with a serrated blade on either side of the handle. The creature, on the other hand, looked similar to a Lavorian, yet black, not silver. It had a crimson eye on each side of its head, and another in the centre of its face above a short snout that dribbled gunk. Spikes covered the entirety of its body from its head to its sharp tail, and the claws on its four paws were like daggers unsheathed.

In front of the Fizorachi and its beast, Dyma and Huadlan floated inside a cage of purple light that was being controlled by the Fizorachi. Every few seconds, a surge of power would course through the cage and torture Dyma's contorted body. Each time, the Fizorachi let out a hideous laugh.

"Leave them alone!" Oracus yelled courageously.

The Fizorachi turned hungrily to Oracus, and he was reminded of the vision he'd had of King Xarmoud. These two creatures looked exactly as they had centuries ago when the Noble War had ended. Oracus remembered the Fizorachi's name was Vlaem, and he was the leader of all the others inhabiting Fervia.

As Vlaem focused on Oracus, the enclosure that had trapped Dyma and Huadlan faded and they fell to the floor. Vlaem aimed his pale hand at Oracus instead, but Oracus shielded himself with Dyma's power and the purple light bounced away harmlessly.

Dyma dragged herself to her feet and drew her sword. "Oracus, we lost the boy," she shouted. "He disappeared and we couldn't find him."

Vlaem rounded on Dyma again and his breath rattled chillingly. "Kill!" was his command.

The three-eyed monster reared onto its hind legs and swiped at Dyma with its sharp claws. A short scream escaped the Rider, but blood soon came and she dropped to the ground.

Oracus stood in shock as Huadlan bellowed in despair. Briefly, the storm came to a halt and the rain ceased to fall, and Oracus's shield evaporated as he lost contact with Dyma's mind. Vlaem stood back and watched with delight as Huadlan limped forwards to hold the body of his dead Rider. Oracus willed her to rise again, but when her Lavorian wept and lost his armour, he knew it was the end.

A pearlescent orb came from Huadlan's chest, rose high into the sky, and showered the clearing with light. Oracus squinted until the orb disappeared, and then he stared mesmerised at the ordinary Orangutan that now crouched in the clearing. With fuzzy orange hair and black hands, feet and face, he looked much different to before, but he was the same grand size he had been. Yet Huadlan was a Lavorian no more. He could no longer speak, and without his armour he was as vulnerable as any other animal of the wild. It was the law of the Riders; he had suffered the same fate as Alticon, Catania's wolf.

Huadlan continued to stroke Dyma's hair and gaze lovingly down at her face until the storm endured. When the winds howled once more, and the rain came down in droves again, he kissed his Rider's forehead and stood up. There was a moment when he considered the Fizorachi, but then he ran forwards to tackle the beast that had executed his Rider.

Inevitably, Vlaem was too fast for an ordinary Orangutan. With swiftness and accuracy, he pierced Huadlan through the heart with his jagged sword. Huadlan sagged to the hilt before he realised his fate. Then his eyes opened wide and he let out a final groan of defeat.

As Vlaem slowly removed his sword from Huadlan's chest and let the dead body flop to the ground, Oracus considered his own attack. But he was alone against a powerful Fizorachi with incredible powers and a monstrous beast at his side. Oracus despised himself for leaving Dyma and Huadlan's bodies, but he had no choice if he wanted to survive. He teleported away from Vlaem, and reappeared where the others were waiting for him.

"They're dead," he said immediately. "Dyma and Huadlan are dead!"

Kivali put her hands to her mouth in disbelief. "No! They can't be."

"Didn't you see Huadlan's orb rise into the sky? They're gone," Oracus said. The reality of it was yet to sink in. "There was nothing I could do."

"What happened?" Kivali asked. She started to run to where Oracus had been but he held her back.

"It's suicide if you go," he said. "It was Vlaem, the Fizorachi leader. His beast killed Dyma and then he killed Huadlan himself."

"No, we have to get their bodies!" Kivali shouted. "We're Riders. We can't just leave!"

"You don't have your powers and I'm not strong enough alone," Oracus said. "Vlaem is really powerful. And Bandor and Onca will be no match for that monster he has with him."

To Oracus's right, a soft spluttering came from the ground and he saw Nivin with his eyes open. He urged Kivali to stay with a tug on her arm, then focused on the young boy.

"Nivin?" he said as he crouched down.

The boy's eyelids fluttered and his breath came in hoarse rasps.

"Don't you dare give up," Oracus ordered. "We can't lose you as well."

Nivin tried to focus on Oracus's face, but his eyes kept rolling backwards. "Mr Oracus?" he said weakly.

"Yes, I'm here."

"It really 'urts, Mr Oracus. Please make it stop 'urtin'."

"Just keep your eyes open," Oracus said. "We'll do what we can." He looked up at Bandor and Kivali, desperate for them to tell him Nivin would be okay. But Kivali was already lost to grief, and Bandor was as stunned as Oracus.

Oracus cradled Nivin's head and the boy coughed feebly, spraying blood onto the collar of his shirt.

"If you *do* have a secret power, then use it to survive this," Oracus pleaded.

Nivin tried to smile, but it made him cough some more.

"Keep fighting," Oracus urged.

As thunder clapped overhead, Oracus wondered if he'd ever felt so helpless. He had accomplished what he came to Fervia for; to rescue Gravaz. But at the cost of three valuable lives.

Oracus grasped Nivin tight and shook him lightly, hoping it would keep him alive. His thoughts turned to when his mother and father had died, both of them drifting into the beyond while he was looking down on them, desperate for them to pull though.

He thought of Jowra next, and then of Vlaem, and considered which of the two was the least daunting to face. But in the end, he couldn't just settle for facing one, he would have to defeat both. And it was irrational to think he actually had a chance of that.

With a war now raging through Pharia like a fire, the fate of the land looked bleak. Oracus would likely lose his own life, as would many of his friends. But one question stood out above all others as he held a bleeding boy in his arms: how many more innocent lives would be lost before Pharia inevitably fell into ruin?

Thank you so much for reading Ice Rider. I am so grateful for you getting this far!

As an indie-author, I rely on readers and their support so I can keep on producing books of high quality. That makes YOU a really important part of my journey.

To help me, please take a moment to add a review. It will honestly mean the world to me. And if you enjoyed the book, I would appreciate it if you could recommend it to anyone you know who may also enjoy it.

It has been my pleasure having you here!

Book 3 of the Oracus Series is available now!

Get *Storm Rider* on your online bookstore.

Printed in Great Britain
by Amazon

78012107R00161